WORLDLY CULTURE IN A HOLY CHURCH

9 SINS INFILTRATING THE CHURCH AND HOW TO BE FREE OF THEM

JANICE BROYLES

WORLDLY CULTURE IN A HOLY CHURCH
By Janice Broyles

Published by Late November Literary
Winston Salem, NC 27107

ISBN (Print): 978-1-7375561-9-0
Copyright 2023 by Janice Broyles
Cover design by Sweet N' Spicy designs
Interior design by Late November Literary

Available in print or online. Visit latenovemberliterary.com.

All rights reserved. No part of this publication may be reproduced in any form without written permission of the publisher, except as provided by the U.S. copyright law.

All Scriptures are taken from the Holy Bible, King James Version (Public Domain), unless otherwise documented and cited.

Library of Congress Cataloging-in-Publication data
Broyles, Janice.
Worldly Culture in a Holy Church / Janice Broyles 1st ed.

Printed in the United States of America

ALSO BY JANICE BROYLES

Other Inspirational Books

by Janice Broyles

No Longer Rejected:

A Woman's Journey from Rejection to Freedom

Expecting Greater:

Aligning Our Desires with God's Will

PRAISE FOR WORLDLY CULTURE IN A HOLY CHURCH

If we are travelling on a road and up ahead there are potholes or if the bridge is out, we would certainly appreciate someone warning us of these hazards. In this work, Janice Broyles gently cautions readers of nine ways in which we as Christians may unwittingly crash and burn. Further, she does not merely spell out danger. She offers direction as to the right way to go. I particularly enjoyed her focus on the fruit of the Spirit. A good read.

~***Dr. David Norris,*** professor at Urshan College and prolific author

Dr. Janice Broyles has provided a great service to sincere believers desperate to be God's church in this generation. Thank you to Janice for your skillful use of scripture to protect God's people from the worldliness that undermines our pursuit of holiness in these last days. This book will be a resource and encouragement to any individual looking for a practical pathway for spiritual growth and victory.

~*Rev. Harold Linder,* pastor of Heavenview United Pentecostal Church

Dedicated to those leaders in the faith who have guided me along the way everlasting

CONTENTS

Foreword	xi
Introduction	xvii

PART ONE
THE SINS OF WORLDLY CULTURE IN A HOLY CHURCH

Chapter 1 *Look at Me*	5
Chapter 2 *Power Pursuit*	21
Chapter 3 *No Room at the Table*	31
Chapter 4 *The Comparison Conundrum*	43
Chapter 5 *Idolatry*	51
Chapter 6 *Apathy*	63
Chapter 7 *The Spirit of Offense*	75
Chapter 8 *The Critical Spirit*	85
Chapter 9 *Gluttony*	95

PART TWO
BIBLICAL INSIGHTS FOR A HOLY CHURCH

Biblical Insight #1:   109
Fruit of the Spirit

Biblical Insight #2:   117
Unity of the Spirit

Biblical Insight #3:   125
Separation from the World

Epilogue   131

Notes   133
Thank you!   135

FOREWORD
REV. CRYSTAL WALLACE

One dictionary defines culture as "the ideas, customs, and social behavior of a particular people or society." Although I was born and raised in eastern Canada, I have been blessed to have lived in five different countries, and to have visited ten others. Consequently, I've been exposed to multiple cultures.

The world becomes much larger, more diverse, and more interesting as you explore varying cultural aspects such as food, language, holidays, social norms, business practices and values that differ from your own. Not only has it been a pleasure to learn about new (to me) cultures, but it's also been a delight to share North American culture with our multicultural friends.

When cultures collide, the impact can be enlightening, pleasant, and funny, or frightening, embarrassing, or even disastrous. My husband and I are living proof of that fact! Trust me, we have absolutely made some faux pas along the way, but thankfully, the collateral damage has been negligent; sometimes hilarious and embarrassing, but negligent! Cultural differences are a fact of life that cannot be avoided, nor ignored.

In the natural, when differing cultures exist side-by-side, it happens that some cultural habits are assimilated by the others. Again, depending on the particular cultural norm, this can be a positive or negative thing. In her book, Janice Broyles discusses nine worldly cultures that today's church is assimilating, and in this case, it is not a positive thing. As Scripture says: "My brother and sisters, this should not be" (James 3:10, NIV.)

Repeatedly, God told Israel to be vigilant about not mixing with the neighboring cultures. Why? Because He knew they would become assimilated into pagan cultures and that they would be turned away from loving and serving Him with their whole heart, mind, soul, and strength. He knew that ultimately, they would "imitate the nations around them, although the Lord had ordered them 'Do not to do as they do'" (2 Kings 17:14, NIV.)

FOREWORD

Scripture is clear about the end result of this mixing of cultures: "So the Lord was very angry with Israel and removed them from his presence" (2 Kings 17:18, NIV.) Then, and now, assimilating worldly culture into a godly life has the final consequence of separation from God.

In her opening remarks, Janice Broyles states that while writing this book, God convicted her "of several areas in [her] life that needed pruning." Admittedly, while reading this book, God was also working on me. The truth is, no matter how long we've been serving God, we all have branches in our lives that need to be pruned. Isaiah 62:6 talks about watchmen being posted on the walls of Jerusalem. That watchman can be in the form of a pastor, teacher, leader, parent, friend…or even a book. But the ultimate authority used by each of these "watchmen" must be the Word of God! The author has included numerous Scriptures to back up her arguments, and each has spoken directly to me!

So now it's your turn. As you read this book, do so with an open heart, and prayerfully ask the Lord to reveal any area in which you might be allowing the culture of this world to creep in. When He does, allow the pruning shears of His Spirit to cut away anything that would not be pleasing in His sight. And here's

FOREWORD

another idea: why not grab a group of friends, put on a large pot of coffee and study the book together? I promise that if you do, it will be time well spent.

*For the word of God is alive and powerful. It is sharper than the sharpest two-edged sword, cutting between soul **[our thoughts, our desires, our feelings and emotions]** and spirit, between joint and marrow. It exposes our innermost thoughts and desires.* (Hebrews 4:12 NLT; **clarification and emphasis mine**)

~Rev. Crystal Wallace, missionary to Belgium and author of the book, *Tea Time Treasures*

Love not the world, neither the things that are in the world. If any man love the world, the love of the Father is not in him.

For all that is in the world, the lust of the flesh, and the lust of the eyes, and the pride of life, is not of the Father, but is of the world.

And the world passeth away, and the lust thereof: but he that doeth the will of God abideth for ever.

1 John 2:15-17

INTRODUCTION
TWO CULTURES COLLIDE

This is a book for the church. It's a wakeup call. But it's more than that. In all transparency, this is a book for me.

I know, I know. A bit ironic since I dive into the subject matter of self-centeredness quite a bit. Just the same, this is a book written as God convicted me of several areas in my life that needed pruning. It was difficult to write the chapters that illustrated how the world's culture reached into the Sunday School classrooms and sanctuaries of our churches because God was whispering how much it had taken root in my own life. I say this because at no point do I want the reader to feel as if the author is pointing a finger. Trust me, worldly culture infected my soul on more than one occasion. The whole "die daily" thing took on a whole new meaning.

Jesus said in John 17:16 that his disciples are not of the world just as he was not of this world. But what does that mean? We must live here. We work and often raise families.

The more I thought about it, the more clarity I needed. "How do I live in this world, yet not love this world? How do I love people, but not the world? How do I serve God and not unintentionally—or intentionally—push people away?"

So many questions. Thankfully, God was and is patient with me. This book is therefore the result of God kindly, lovingly revealing His ways. I do not profess to know or understand it all, but I pray that you read this book with an open heart to truly hear what the Word of God says to the church, to you, and to me.

Have you ever looked up at the night's stars and marveled? Or sat on the sand watching the ocean's waves and taking in the sea air? Or hiked a forest trail and appreciated the beauty around you? I have. God's creation is awe-inspiring. This planet we inhabit showcases the splendor of our Creator.

Mankind too shows the incredible vastness of God's talent. Created in his image, we live and have dominion on the earth. With this comes the gift of freewill, and it is here we falter and fall short. Since Adam and Eve's sin, kingdoms have been built despite man's misguided ways. Through the rise and fall of empires, communities have grown and thrived together, establishing their own rules of that specific society.

We are all a part of these communities or cultures. Culture is one's customs and social institutions that shape the knowledge, beliefs, and ideals of their group. There are also subcultures within cultures. And we belong to many: our family's culture, our country's culture, our school's culture, our church's culture, etc.

The Culture of a Holy Church

God's Word establishes kingdom culture. It is his kingdom, and with that, he specifies how we ought to act and think. Satan's main objective has been to sabotage this, and in so doing, establish a counterculture to God's perfect design. This can be observed in Scripture.

- First, through His creation, God created order. Everything has a purpose.
- When sin disrupted the divine order, God already had a plan to restore it and bring his beloved creation back to Him.
- God called to Abram and through him created a nation whose God is the Lord.
- Once again, sin disrupted God's plan. Through Abraham's disobedience, his seed brought about two races of humanity, both at war with each other.
- Through Isaac's son Jacob came the 12 tribes of Israel, and these tribes flourished in Egypt, growing into the millions. However, the Old Testament documents their continued struggle between living a holy life before God or following the desires of their flesh.
- Even though Jesus came and paid the price for our sins, this daily struggle of flesh versus spirit rages on today in each of us.

Make no mistake, God's church *must* be holy. How

can this happen when our righteousness is as filthy rags (Isaiah 64:6)? Through his grace, mercy, and compassion, he offers redemption through his blood and leads and guides us toward this finished product. We are not there yet, but we understand the biblical commands and must fight to keep the church holy in today's culture.

- A holy church loves God and loves their neighbor.
- A holy church follows the commandments of Christ.
- A holy church is born again of water and spirit.
- A holy church establishes itself on the unshakeable foundation of the Word.
- A holy church separates itself from the world.

The Culture of the World

Worldly culture is the customs, traditions, and institutions of this world. It looks at life through a different lens than that of the kingdom of God.

- Worldly culture emphasizes personal pleasures.
- Worldly culture emphasizes self-centeredness.
- Worldly culture emphasizes pride.
- Worldly culture emphasizes individualized significance.
- Worldly culture emphasizes comparisons and competition.

The Clashing of these Two Worldviews

Worldly culture and kingdom culture are not the same. Worldly culture promotes self while Jesus commands we deny ourselves, take up our cross, and follow Him (Luke 9:23). Worldly culture says if it feels good, do it, yet the Word says there is a way that seems right to man, but it ends in death (Proverbs 14:12).

These two world views clash. There is no merging of these ideas and lifestyles. Jesus warned of this in Matthew 6:24: "No man can serve two masters: for either he will hate the one, and love the other; or else he will hold to the one, and despise the other..." Trying to embrace both cultures results in a tepid, watered-down gospel. In Revelation 3:16, Jesus is clear about the results of a water-downed gospel: "So then because thou art lukewarm, and neither cold nor hot, I will spue thee out of my mouth."

Yet, more and more, believers look and act like the world, using the world's standards as the measuring stick for the church. The lines, not surprisingly, have become blurred.

Pastors and church leadership feel the effects of this mentality as their congregants struggle with obeying the Word of God because they no longer *know* the Word of God. Scriptural illiteracy plagues us as the masses profess Christ with their mouths but do not seek Him first in their hearts.

- Only 11% of Americans read the Bible daily with over 50% never reading it. Yet 70% of Americans still identify as Christian.[1]

So, who's reading their Bible? The answer is only a few.

The reasons are multi-factorial, but they mostly fall into the category of too many distractions or too many excuses. For these reasons, we have let the culture of the world infiltrate the church so much so that the church is often a reflection of the world in which it lives.

INTRODUCTION

- Don't tell me what to do.
- Don't tell me how to dress.
- Don't tell me how to live.
- Make me feel good, or I won't come back.
- Entertain me but don't convict me.

Some argue that the Bible tells us to work out our own salvation, and we don't need other people telling us what to do. But we neglect the entire verse of Philippians 2:12: "Wherefore, my beloved, as ye have always obeyed, not as in my presence only, but now much more in my absence, work out your own salvation with fear and trembling." Paul was not present with them, so he was encouraging them to study the Word for themselves. Paul was not saying that the Philippians didn't have to attend church anymore or that they didn't need Godly leadership in their lives. Nor does this mean that working out our own salvation implies that there are multiple ways to earn it. He was entrusting them to continue in obedience in the faith and to work out their salvation "with fear and trembling." This means with a holy reverence and awe. But if we're not even reading the Word, much less doing so in reverence and awe, then we are not correctly obeying this verse. And in John 17:17, there is a simple reason why we must read and study the

Word: "Sanctify them through thy truth: thy word is truth." If we want the truth, we must stop looking to this worldly culture and instead turn to the truth of the Word of God. A holy church's foundation must be built on this truth.

Why This Book? Why Now?

I have read Matthew 23 several times in my walk with God, yet as I studied this chapter, my eyes were opened to the struggles of my flesh that were impacting my walk with God and my relationship with others.

> *Woe unto you, scribes and Pharisees, hypocrites! for ye pay tithe of mint and anise and cummin, and have omitted the weightier matters of the law, judgment, mercy, and faith: these ought ye to have done, and not to leave the other undone. Ye blind guides, which strain at a gnat, and swallow a camel. Woe unto you, scribes and Pharisees, hypocrites!* ***for ye make clean the outside of the cup and of the platter, but within they are full of extortion and excess****. Thou blind Pharisee, cleanse first that which is within the cup and platter, that the outside of them may be clean also. Woe unto you, scribes and Pharisees, hypocrites!* ***for ye are like unto whited***

sepulchres, which indeed appear beautiful outward, but are within full of dead men's bones, and of all uncleanness. **Even so ye also outwardly appear righteous unto men, but within ye are full of hypocrisy and iniquity.** Woe unto you, scribes and Pharisees, hypocrites! because ye build the tombs of the prophets, and garnish the sepulchres of the righteous, And say, If we had been in the days of our fathers, we would not have been partakers with them in the blood of the prophets. Wherefore ye be witnesses unto yourselves, that ye are the children of them which killed the prophets. Fill ye up then the measure of your fathers. Ye serpents, ye generation of vipers, how can ye escape the damnation of hell? (Matthew 23:23-32)

The scribes and Pharisees were the religious people of their time, but I abhorred the thought of comparing myself to them. Surely, I was not that bad. Then I read Jesus's warnings to the seven churches in Revelation. Several of them had fallen short of the glorious church they were meant to be. It got me thinking: in what ways is today's church struggling? Could it be that we love the world and its culture? Do we love our luxuries and our delicacies more than our relationship with Jesus?

The challenge is not only due to falling short of

the glory of God because we all have. It is turning a blind eye to certain sins and letting them manifest in our congregations and in our own lives. Paul poses the question in Romans 6:1-2:

> *What shall we say then? Shall we continue in sin, that grace may abound? God forbid. How shall we, that are dead to sin, live any longer therein?*

There is no such thing as *acceptable sin*. Sin is sin. It is disobedience to the will and authority of God, and if we don't change our ways, not only could the church flounder, but lost souls may face eternal damnation because we neglected to be the light God called us to be.

- The world needs a holy church to shine through the darkness.
- God is coming back for a bride without spot or blemish.
- Choosing to come out from among the world opens the door to the supernatural.

God's way is the only way. If we are to be a holy church, we must recognize worldly culture and drive it out of our lives. How can we be a city on a hill when

INTRODUCTION

we are no longer standing upon the rock but are building our foundation upon sinking sand? God help us recognize the lies of the enemy and clean up our own lives so that we can lead others to Him before it's too late.

PART ONE
THE SINS OF WORLDLY CULTURE IN A HOLY CHURCH

Because my people hath forgotten me, they have burned incense to vanity, and they have caused them to stumble in their ways from the ancient paths, to walk in paths, in a way not cast up;

Jeremiah 18:15

1
LOOK AT ME

Children model what they see and observe, and I was no exception. My favorite game of pretend was lining up my stuffed animals and dolls and "having church" in our basement.

When I was a young teen, I often had the chore of cleaning the kitchen. I hated it more than the other chores. One way I got through the dirty dishes was by grabbing an available utensil (spatulas or whisks worked the best) and using it as a microphone. I would then sing and preach at my reflection in the microwave. This was long before cell phones or selfies, but there was something enjoyable about imaginative play or fantasizing about the "What if…"

Children playing pretend is an important part of their learning, growing, and adapting into their culture. However, with the advent of the cell phone and handheld technology came a whirlwind of side effects. Research says that many people today struggle with reality and would much rather live in their fantasy worlds.[1] And this is the world in which we're raising our children. It's a world that promotes self.

It makes sense. In our minds, we're the main character of the story. In our fantasies, we're the star of the show. Shouldn't the world revolve around us?

This flawed thinking hurts the church because it takes our focus off God and places it on ourselves. Lifting each other up and encouraging one another are both Godly and required of a holy church. Satan's tactic is to make God's people hunger for flattery in such a way that vanity plants itself into the soil of our hearts. Vanity corrupts.

The *look at me* culture has infiltrated the church, thanks to the megaphone platforms within our circles and online. The proverbial saint and sinner alike bask in the attention received from selfies. Church services end only for modeling sessions to begin. We take pictures of ourselves in our cars, eating meals, out with friends, working out, sitting on the couch, or reading a book. When did it become socially acceptable to take a picture of oneself in a bathroom mirror?

With the popularity of Tiktok, the picture frenzy turned into a video craze. Recording ourselves singing, dancing, or eating has become more the norm than outlier behavior.

Why?

The answer is simple. *We want attention.*

More than that, we crave it to the point that it becomes an idol. Psalm 119:37 says, "Turn away mine eyes from beholding vanity; and quicken thou me in thy way." This means that vanity does not follow the way of God. Proverbs 31:30 warns to not seek favor or pursue beauty: "Favour is deceitful, and beauty is vain…"

Often, selfies and highlighting our looks—whether through social media or face-to-face communication—are intended to draw attention and favor to ourselves, yet the Word says that it is deceitful, which means we are only fooling ourselves. Let's explore this further.

The Sin of Vanity

When does our appreciation of kind words and compliments give way to sin? When do our talents become a stumbling block?

First, it's important to note that taking pictures

of family and fun times is not inherently sinful. Today's social media allows families to stay connected. There's also a benefit of today's technology in that we are reaching all parts of the world with our gospel message. There have been many sermons that have spoken to me, encouraged me, and convicted me, even though I wasn't present in the service. During the recent pandemic, streaming songs and sermons were needed to bring church services and special messages into our homes. All these examples continue to allow the gospel to be preached around the globe and right into people's devices.

Satan isn't going to sit back and let that happen. As is his way, he sneakily twists and perverts our noble, Godly intentions. Just like with Eve, he tempts the individual and uses our search for significance and purpose against us to lure us to a place of pride and vain glory. As Peter writes in 1 Peter 5:8, "Be sober, be vigilant, because your adversary the devil, as a roaring lion, walketh about, seeking whom he may devour."

It *is* a slippery slope because vanity *is* a sin. Vanity is a *heart* condition. It is simply pride manifesting itself in self-centeredness (we'll take a deeper look at pride in the next chapter). If not careful, vanity becomes an open door to hedonism, lasciviousness, and immorality. According to 2 Peter 2:18, it says:

> *For when they speak great swelling words of vanity, they allure through the lusts of the flesh, through much wantonness, those that were clean escaped from them who live in error.*

As this verse indicates, vanity not only hurts the one who is vain, but it allures others through lust of their flesh. For example, we want to look good. Why? Is it simply pride in one's appearance, or is it more than that? Are we trying to come across as alluring? Are we trying to appear desirable to others to provoke lust or envy?

Seeking vain glory is also sinful. Jesus explains:

> *And when thou prayest, thou shalt not be as the hypocrites are: for they love to pray standing in the synagogues and in the corners of the streets, that* **they may be seen of men.** *Verily I say unto you,* **They have their reward.** *But thou, when thou prayest, enter into thy closet, and when thou hast shut thy door,* **pray to thy Father which is in secret;** *and thy Father which seeth in secret shall reward thee openly. But when ye pray,* **use not vain repetitions,** *as the*

heathen do: ***for they think that they shall be heard for their much speaking.*** (Matthew 6:5-7; **emphasis mine**)

Jesus pointedly calls out those who stand in synagogues and on street corners bringing attention to themselves for being "spiritual." He is not impressed, calling them hypocrites. Instead of drawing attention to ourselves so that we look good to others (even in our spiritual endeavors), we should pray and serve others in secret. This means that we shouldn't seek attention for these things. When we do so, we have received the only reward we will get, and that is the attention of others. If we are seeking man's approval for our spirituality, then we are participating in the sin of vanity. God is not impressed, nor does he approve.

In worldly culture, humanity has become its own god. The ideology of "the self" screams from the rooftops of our culture. "Look at me! Look at me!" Think about it. Vanity promotes oneself. It takes God off the throne of our hearts and places ourselves there instead. Our flesh thrives on flattery and attention, and in a world that promotes influencers and vain pursuits, self-centeredness has become a spiritual epidemic.

What makes vanity so distasteful in God's eyes? The answer comes down to flesh versus spirit.

Vanity prioritizes our flesh and self-interests. With vanity, we are being ruled by our flesh and not the Spirit.

- Galatians 5:24-26 gives more clarity: "And they that are Christ's have crucified the flesh with the affections and lusts. If we live in the Spirit, let us also walk in the Spirit. Let us not be desirous of vain glory, provoking one another, envying one another."

Vanity leads us down the wrong path, which has dire consequences.

- "I have seen all the works that are done under the sun; and, behold, all is vanity and vexation of spirit. That which is crooked cannot be made straight: and that which is wanting cannot be numbered" (Ecclesiastes 1:14-15).

Vanity is rooted in insecurity.

- "For all his days are sorrows, and his travail grief; yea, his heart taketh not rest in the night. This is also vanity" (Ecclesiastes 2:23).

Vanity blinds us to the ways of God because our focus is no longer on Him.

- "This I say therefore and testify in the Lord that ye henceforth walk not as other Gentiles walk in the ***vanity of their mind.*** Having the understanding darkened, being alienated from the life of God through the ignorance that is in them, because of the ***blindness of their heart***" (Ephesians 4:17-18; ***emphasis mine***).

Vanity is bedfellows with other spiritual ailments: jealousy, idolatry, pride, hedonism, comparisons, envy, and strife, all of which are sin. When we get distracted by our own wants and pleasures, we are enticed by it—we are drawn into its pleasures—which conceives and bears sin, ultimately leading to our spiritual death.

- "But every man is tempted, when he is drawn away of his own lust, and enticed. Then when lust hath conceived, it bringeth forth sin: and sin, when it is finished, bringeth forth death. Do not err, my beloved brethren" (James 1:14-16).

Vanity is deceitful, puffing us up. This superficially elevates us above others, which drives comparisons and negative feelings.

- "...vainly puffed up by his fleshly mind" (Colossians 2:18).
- "And when thou art spoiled, what wilt thou do? Though thou clothest thyself with crimson, though thou deckest thee with ornaments of gold, though thou rentest thy face with painting, in vain shalt thou make thyself fair; thy lovers will despise thee, they will seek thy life" (Jeremiah 4:30).

Vanity's Stronghold

Once vanity is rooted in our lives, it builds a stronghold and leads to other sins: lust of the flesh, lust of the eye, and pride of life are all rooted in vain glory and self-centeredness. In biblical context, lust does not necessarily mean "sexual lust," but lust is any sinful longing that is contrary to God and his will.

When examining it in this context, lust of the flesh involves any longings that satisfy the flesh. This could be sexual longings, but it could also be feeding our flesh in other ways. Lust of the flesh is living a life dominated by extremes that satisfy the senses—sight, hearing, taste, touch, and smell—which includes feeding into pleasure, gratifying through material possessions, and pursuing hedonism even at the expense of others. Since the flesh is contrary to the Spirit, the lust of the flesh is rebellion against God.

Lust of the eye is desiring what we see. The outward show of possessions, looks, and materialism becomes our god. It is the principal component to covetousness. We long for what others have, or we lust after opulent lifestyles, and we revel in ourselves when we "get there." Once again, lust of the eye can refer to sexual lust, but Jesus tells us in Matthew 6:23: "But if thine eye be evil, thy whole body shall be full of darkness…" Spiritually speaking, our eyes are connected to our hearts, which is why we must guard our eyes from anything that goes against the Word of God.

We would be lying if we said we didn't look at the outward appearance of a person. Of course, we do (and the Bible says we do). The lust of the eye is a major stumbling block in our lives. We enjoy visually appealing items and individuals. If not controlled, this leads to covetousness, which is idolatry (Colossians 3:5). Furthermore, we should not desire anyone to look at us in such a way.

Lastly, the pride of life is simply the promotion of ourselves or the embracing of the arrogance found in self-sufficiency. The pride of life is the desire for recognition, accolades, and status, and it promotes competition. With the pride of life, we place ourselves above others or compare ourselves to those whom we see as above ourselves. The pride of life is vanity and keeps our attention on our surroundings and not on our Savior.

All three of these sins are interconnected and become strongholds. Our desire for attention stems from the pride of life, which leads to the lust of the eye, which is desiring what others have, whether it's their outward appearances, their talents, or their lifestyles. We continue in the lust of the flesh by fulfilling these desires. Unfortunately, these lusts are insatiable, and when we feed them, enough is never enough. Thus, this creates a stronghold.

Biblical Warnings

The Bible reminds us that "the Lord seeth not as man seeth; for man looketh on the outward appearance, but the Lord looketh on the heart" (1 Samuel 16:7). When he examines our hearts, does he see a stronghold rooted in vanity or vain glory? Does he see us coveting what others have? Does he see our desires for popularity and power? Does he see jealousy?

The Word of God does not mince words when it comes to denouncing vanity or vain glory.

- "Do ye look on things after the outward appearance? if any man trust to himself that he is Christ's, let him of himself think this again, that, as he is Christ's, even so are we Christ's" (2 Corinthians 10:7).
- "For the grace of God that bringeth salvation hath appeared to all men, Teaching us that, denying ungodliness and worldly lusts, we should live soberly, righteously, and godly, in this present world" (Titus 2:11-12)
- "Take heed that ye do not your alms before men, to be seen of them: otherwise ye have **no reward** of your Father which is

in heaven. Therefore when thou doest thine alms, do not sound a trumpet before thee, as the hypocrites do in the synagogues and in the streets, that ***they may have glory of men.*** Verily I say unto you, ***They have their reward***. But when thou doest alms, let not thy left hand know what thy right hand doeth: That thine alms may be in secret: and ***thy Father which seeth in secret himself shall reward thee openly***" (Matthew 6:1-4; ***emphasis mine***).

- "For though we walk in the flesh, we do not war after the flesh: (For the weapons of our warfare are not carnal, but mighty through God to the pulling down of strong holds;) Casting down imaginations, and ***every high thing that exalteth itself*** against the knowledge of God, and ***bringing into captivity every thought to the obedience of Christ***" (2 Corinthians 10:3-5; ***emphasis mine***).
- "This I say then, Walk in the Spirit, and ye shall not fulfil the lust of the flesh. For the flesh lusteth against the Spirit, and the Spirit against the flesh: and ***these are***

contrary the one to the other: so that ye cannot do the things that ye would" (Galatians 5:16-17; *emphasis mine*).
- "Mortify therefore your members which are upon the earth; fornication, uncleanness, inordinate affection, evil concupiscence, and covetousness, which is idolatry: For which things' sake ***the wrath of God cometh on the children of disobedience:*** In the which ye also walked some time, when ye lived in them" (Colossians 3:5-7; *emphasis mine*).
- "And base things of the world, and things which are despised, hath God chosen, yea, and things which are not, to ***bring to nought*** things that are: ***That no flesh should glory in his presence***" (1 Corinthians 1:28-29; *emphasis mine*).

The Bible warns us to turn away from vanity and instead turn to Christ. When our focus is stayed on him, we decrease, and he increases.

Final Thoughts

Our desire for attention and outward affirmation

takes our attention off God and our relationship with Him. And if He slips from the number one spot in our lives, then we have erred.

Vanity has no place in God's presence; therefore, it has no place in the church. Lucifer was kicked out of heaven for pride or vain glory. He wasn't receiving enough attention, which turned into the wicked desire of taking God's place. This led to pursuing power and placing himself—or the opinion of himself—over worship to his Creator. When we try to promote ourselves above others, or when we try to solicit attention to ourselves to elevate our position or perceived value, are we not acting like Lucifer?

Let's set the selfie stick down and stop trying to promote ourselves. It isn't about the "likes" or "follows." It isn't about how popular we are, how others see us, or how much attention we are given. It's about Jesus and his saving grace. When he truly gets the glory in our lives, we tap into his presence and power. When we stop promoting ourselves and start promoting the Gospel, the church will be unstoppable.

2

POWER PURSUIT

As a writer, I have been counseled many times by literary agents and editors that I need to build my platform to see success. I've always struggled with this advice because it goes against my spirit. I'm not comfortable promoting myself. With books, my name is on each jacket. So, yes, I desire readers to purchase my books and enjoy them, but how far am I willing to go to make that happen? More so, how far are any of us willing to go to build a platform for ourselves?

Pursuing power and influence is often considered normal human behavior. When my son was younger, he had to clean his room before he could play outside. While in his room, he muttered, "I can't wait until I'm old, then I won't have to be told what to do!" He saw me as powerful because I asserted my authority as his mother. In his mind, once he became an adult, he too would be powerful.

Think about who we see as powerful. When we were children, we often saw parents and teachers as powerful. They held the authority in our lives. As working adults, we learned quickly how the world worked. Government officials hold certain power. Bosses or managers hold some power over us. When we're "people pleasers," even strangers can hold some power over us!

Our current world's culture also places high value on those who are "influencers." Social media is full of individuals who have millions of followers and who influence the culture toward certain behaviors, attitudes, and lifestyles. If we're not careful, it is easy to get sucked into this worldly frame of mind.

Power and influence propel people forward. With power comes influence and authority. This gives people favor and special attention. It doesn't take long for us to desire it. My sons approached me one Christmas and decided that they needed at least ten presents under the tree. The idea put a smile on my face, but I did not agree with their proposal. Since I had the power in that situation, I did not have to do what they proposed.

Each of us has our opinions, but when a person

has no power or authority, then others may not value the opinion given. No one enjoys being powerless, but if we're honest, there are times when we all feel that way. Craving power and authority can have a hold on our hearts, so much so that we will promote ourselves in a way that gives us perceived authority.

In the spiritual sense, God is all-powerful, and there is nothing wrong with pursuing him. He desires us to "draw nigh" to him (James 4:8). Tapping into faith, learning to trust in God through the storms of life, and surrendering to his will are a few of the ways to usher the power of God into our lives. Sadly, what's crept into our churches is the pursuit of power through pride. Feeling significant in our church services and fellowships makes us feel good.

In what ways do we feel significant? We feel significant when we are promoted or patted on the back, or we feel significant when stepping into a position of authority. But will we continue to serve God if we never get that pat on the back? Will we harbor offense if we don't receive that position of power or authority?

Pursuing power and the influence that comes with it for selfish gain or to feel significant is pride and self-centeredness. It goes against the will of God, and it inhibits spiritual growth. God cannot work freely in our lives when we are our own gods. A holy church must not search for significance in a way that glorifies or promotes ourselves, yet this is a common struggle for saints and sinners alike.

The Sin of Pride

In worldly culture, pursuing power is a necessity to "get ahead." Pride is celebrated and even pushed on young children. Our desire for accolades starts young. Children may show their parents something they colored and say, "See it? Isn't it beautiful?" This is human nature. Many of us feel loved and accepted by positive words and encouragement. This is not inherently sinful. It's when we seek it out and become self-inflated with pride that it becomes sinful.

As is Satan's way, he perverts this human appreciation for kindness and accolades into promoting ourselves to the point that our ego needs to be stroked. Jesus spoke sternly against pursuing power: "...the last shall be first, and the first last..." (Matthew 20:16). Pride deceptively elevates us above others. Pride promotes self and pursues power. It's important to remember that God hates pride.

Pride is sinful not only when we use it to exalt

ourselves above others but also when we abuse any power or influence we've obtained to hurt or manipulate people. In the church it may look like telling someone "God told me…" when really, it is an assertion of our will and has nothing to do with God. Another example may be judging someone and outwardly condemning them for not doing things our way. "Church hurt" is very real, and this trauma normally occurs when someone else abuses their power or influence. God forbid we ever behave in such a way.

Pride's Stronghold

Pride's stronghold is detrimental in our walk with God. It is a hunger for attention or individual significance and places self above all else. It is a form of worship where we place our desires and interests first. As discussed in the previous chapter, it is connected with vanity and seeks vain glory. What does pride look like in our lives?

- Any action that promotes ourselves
- Desiring the spotlight or being the center of attention

- Needing others' affirmations and accolades to stay content and feel important
- Living in a state of offense when things don't go our way
- Becoming upset when others are chosen but not us
- Comparing ourselves with others and being jealous when others are perceived as better
- Sowing discord to make others look bad

Pride's stronghold tears down relationships and creates discontent. Its manifestation in the church leads to church splits, quarrels among the brethren, cliquish and exclusionary behaviors, performing instead of praising, prejudices and ungodly biases, and disgruntled members. Satan wants pride in the church. He glories in our discontent and grumblings. He thrives on our competitiveness and pursuit of power. He relishes our arguments and gossip. When pride is a stronghold, we open wide the doors for the devil himself to walk in and wreak havoc.

Biblical Warnings

The Word of God has a few things to say about pursuing power and influence through pride. In 1 Samuel 15:23, it says that rebellion (pride) is "as the sin of witchcraft."

- "And whosoever shall exalt himself shall be abased" (Matthew 23:12).
- "…Wherefore he saith, God resisteth the proud, but giveth grace unto the humble" (James 4:6).
- "The fear of the Lord is to hate evil: pride, and arrogancy, and the evil way, and the froward mouth, do I hate" (Proverbs 8:13).
- "Talk no more so exceeding proudly; **let not arrogancy come out of your mouth**: for the Lord is a God of knowledge, and **by him actions are weighed**" (1 Samuel 2:3; **emphasis mine**).
- "Pride goeth before destruction, and an haughty spirit before a fall" (Proverbs 16:18).
- "For I say, through the grace given unto me, to every man that is among you, **not to think of himself more highly than he**

***ought to think*;** but to think soberly, according as God hath dealt to every man the measure of faith" (Romans 12:3; **emphasis mine).**

Let us heed the Word of God and purge ourselves of pride. The antidote is simple: "Humble yourselves therefore under the mighty hand of God, that he may exalt you in due time" (1 Peter 5:6).

Final Thoughts

There is nothing like when the Word goes forth in a church service or a Bible study in one's home, hearts are convicted, and lives are changed. I grew up on the church pew, and I am honored to have heard some of the greatest sermons ever delivered. Men and women of God have spoken into my life in ways that have forever changed me.

But I've also witnessed the other side of ministry:

- The crushing weight of people's opinions and demands
- The juggle of balancing ministry with family and work duties

- The late-night panicked phone calls and hospital visits
- The church member offended, vowing never to return
- The flattery of someone with impure intentions

Real ministry is not glamorous nor is it full of accolades. It's Bible studies, Sunday School classes, and jail visits. It's knocking on doors and late-night prayer requests. It's service to one another.

It annoys me that Satan has twisted the definition and design of ministry to self-service and an ambitious pursuit of power. When it becomes more about who sees us and less about who sees Christ in us, then it is sin. As stated earlier: He must increase; we must decrease. Pride cannot have a place in God's holy church.

3

NO ROOM AT THE TABLE

Friends are friends forever when the Lord's the Lord of them[1]...*but* what about the new convert? What about the guest sitting in the back of the church that doesn't look like you? Can they be your friend too?

This is a hard chapter for me to write. I say this because I have struggled with rejection for most of my life. I was the one who didn't receive the invitation, who was told that I wasn't wanted in their circle of friends, who was ignored or picked on. I was told that I was annoying and that I talked too much. And even though I did experience rejection in the world, the above examples happened within the church.

Now that I'm an adult, I understand the nuances of familiarity and comfort within groups. I don't expect an invitation to everything. I understand that not everyone will like me.

But there are many within our churches who are still learning and growing in Christ. They may not have fully developed spiritual maturity, specifically children, teens, and new converts. When these individuals see cliques or hear about parties and after church get-togethers they are not invited to, they may feel unwelcomed or unloved within the family of believers. Even the most seasoned saint can struggle with feeling rejected when ignored or isolated.

This can be tricky to navigate because there are those we make friends with easily, and inviting everyone may be an overwhelming situation. Finding this balance is vital to a healthy church because there is never an excuse to exclude someone from friendship and brotherly—or sisterly—charity and fellowship. Cliquish behaviors and exclusionary actions have no place in God's holy church.

This is evident throughout Jesus's ministry. He went out of his way to minister to those who were outsiders. He fellowshipped with publicans and tax collectors. Out of a large crowd, he chose to approach Zaccheus, a despised tax collector, and joined him for a meal. He rebuked those who were critical of Mary Magdalene. He waited at the well to meet the one woman no one else liked. He chose disciples from all walks of life. He spoke this parable about a rich man lacking kindness and compassion for his fellow man:

> *There was a rich man who was dressed in purple and fine linen and lived in luxury every day. At his gate was laid a beggar named Lazarus, covered with sores and longing to eat what fell from the rich man's table. Even the dogs came and licked his sores. "The time came when the beggar died and the angels carried him to Abraham's side. The rich man also died and was buried. In Hades, where he was in torment, he looked up and saw Abraham far away, with Lazarus by his side. So he called to him, 'Father Abraham, have pity on me and send Lazarus to dip the tip of his finger in water and cool my tongue, because I am in agony in this fire.' "But Abraham replied, 'Son, remember that in your lifetime you received your good things, while Lazarus received bad things, but now he is comforted here and you are in agony. (Luke 16:19-25 NIV)*

In this parable, the rich man was blessed with riches and lived in luxury, yet he did not help the beggar at his gate. He lacked compassion and refused to extend fellowship with Lazarus. When he died, he was judged for it. Some may argue that he was judged for being rich, but Abraham himself was a rich man, yet the parable places him in a place offering comfort to Lazarus. Jesus's point goes even deeper than a warning against greed and selfishness. It's a warning not to turn our backs on those we may overlook or who we judge as beneath us. According to this parable, we will have to answer for these actions.

Most of us have encountered those who have left the church because they felt isolated or that they "didn't belong." These individuals may be wrong in their perception and justification, but we may not be exempt from wrongdoing. In God's kingdom, we should endeavor to make sure we exhibit the fruit of the Spirit with everyone we meet.

The Sin of Exclusion

> This might have you scratching your head. How is excluding others sinful? What happens if I simply forget to invite someone, or what if I don't make enough money to help every homeless person I encounter? Remember that God examines the heart. Purposeful exclusion, lacking compassion toward our fellow man, or being so focused on ourselves and our own happiness that we neglect serving

others are manifestations of a heart issue. Jesus explained it best in Matthew 25:34-45:

Then shall the King say unto them on his right hand, Come, ye blessed of my Father, inherit the kingdom prepared for you from the foundation of the world: For I was an hungred, and ye gave me meat: I was thirsty, and ye gave me drink: I was a stranger, and ye took me in: Naked, and ye clothed me: I was sick, and ye visited me: I was in prison, and ye came unto me. Then shall the righteous answer him, saying, Lord, when saw we thee an hungred, and fed thee? or thirsty, and gave thee drink? When saw we thee a stranger, and took thee in? or naked, and clothed thee? Or when saw we thee sick, or in prison, and came unto thee? And the King shall answer and say unto them, **Verily I say unto you, Inasmuch as ye have done it unto one of the least of these my brethren, ye have done it unto me.**

Then shall he say also unto them on the left hand, Depart from me, ye cursed, into everlasting fire, prepared for the devil and his angels: For I was an hungred, and ye gave me no meat: I was thirsty, and ye gave me no drink: I was a stranger, and ye took me not in: naked, and ye clothed me not: sick, and in prison, and ye visited me not. Then shall they also answer him, saying, Lord, when saw we thee an hungred, or athirst, or a stranger, or naked, or sick, or in prison, and did not minister unto thee? Then shall he answer them, saying, **Verily I say unto you, Inasmuch as ye did it not to one of the least of these, ye did it not to me.** *(emphasis mine)*

Purposeful exclusion displeases God. In the verses above, we see the consequence for ignoring the hungry, the needy, the sick, and the reprobate, which is to be cursed and thrown into "everlasting fire." On the other hand, serving "the least of these" reaps an inheritance into the kingdom of God. These needy individuals come from all walks of life, and many who are needy attend our churches. We cannot assume that because someone doesn't look like they need help or fellowship that they are fine. Appearances can be deceiving. Offering compassion and brotherly love should extend to everyone.

The biblical example of Mary Magdalene illustrates the beauty and power of Jesus's inclusion of her. This woman didn't fit in, and she made those around her uncomfortable. She was sinful, yet Jesus delivered her. She began to follow him, which probably bothered his other followers. Why was Jesus letting this prostitute follow him?

When Mary Magdalene poured the expensive oil on Jesus's feet and worshipped him, those at his table rebuked her. Their discomfort was clearly seen. This harlot woman did not fit into their circles. They criticized her, but Jesus quickly put them in their place. Her worship and sacrifice moved him because he saw the genuine gratitude of her heart. When the disciples were scattered at the crucifixion, this same woman never left the scene, and she was one of the women who first saw the resurrected Jesus. His inclusion of this flawed woman, among others, showed his love for all, regardless of background and past circumstances. And her love for her Savior was unmatched. Today's church should be no different.

In the world, cliques naturally form because we are social beings who crave like-mindedness and relationships. We naturally gravitate to those like us. There is comfort and familiarity with friend groups. Some of the most anxiety-ridden circumstances involve being in new situations without knowing anyone. This is disconcerting for most of us.

The same can be said of relationships and bonding within the church. Masses of humanity attend church services, and even with the commonality of Christ, we still tend to gravitate to those who best fit our circle. However, this goes against what

God requires of his children. In Matthew 28:19, each of us is commanded to "Go ye therefore, and teach all nations..." How can that happen if we never venture out of our circles? If we are not purposeful in our interactions daily, we may fall short in this area.

The Stronghold of Comfort

What are we doing to make the guest, the outsider, and the prodigal loved and welcomed in the house of God and in the community of believers? What are we doing to teach our children to love all the children in their classes? How are we modeling Christ's love and fellowship to our teenagers? Some may argue that it's not our job, but if we don't do it, who will?

Cliques are created for our comfort. In and of themselves, cliques are exclusive. Some have what it takes to join the "club," while others don't. We get to "choose" who we want in our friend circle, and there is a certain power with that. Yet when we behave this way, we are not behaving like Jesus. The stronghold of comfort focuses on serving ourselves. We don't prefer to step out of our comfort zones. Unfortunately, this leads to limiting interactions with those to whom we wouldn't normally associate.

When this stronghold is within the church, discord and apathy can result. How can there be unity when we do not have a heart for service but for comfort? How can outsiders feel welcomed when we're too busy judging them by our fleshly standards of inclusion?

Biblical Warnings

Kindness requires action (Ephesians 4:32). It is being considerate and empathetic toward others. It is truly serving those without thought to oneself.

- "Now I beseech you, brethren, by the name of our Lord Jesus Christ, that ye all speak the same thing, and that ***there be no divisions among you…***" (1 Corinthians 1:10; ***emphasis mine***).
- "If ye fulfil the royal law according to the scripture, Thou shalt love thy neighbour as thyself, ye do well: But ***if ye have respect to persons, ye commit sin,*** and are convinced of the law as transgressors" (James 2:8-9; ***emphasis mine***).
- "And Jesus knew their thoughts, and said unto them, Every kingdom divided against

itself is brought to desolation; and ***every city or house divided against itself shall not stand***" (Matthew 12:25; ***emphasis mine)***.

- "And these things, brethren... that ye might learn in us ***not to think of men above that which is written***, that ***no one of you be puffed up for one against another***" (1 Corinthians 4:6; ***emphasis mine)***.
- "And the servant of the Lord must not strive ***(be in conflict);*** but be gentle unto all men, apt to teach, patient" (2 Timothy 2:24; ***clarification mine***).
- "I have shewed you all things, how that so labouring ye ought to ***support the weak***, and to remember the words of the Lord Jesus, how he said, ***It is more blessed to give than to receive"*** (Acts 20:35; ***emphasis mine***).

Final Thoughts

Jesus died for every single human being. No one was excluded. If Jesus loves us so much that he invited "whosoever will" to partake in his salvation, we too must be open to reaching and loving everyone, even those who wouldn't normally fit in with us.

- This means becoming conscientious about our interactions at church and in our daily lives.
- It means being purposeful in our conversations and inclusive in our gatherings.
- It means inviting guests to your Sunday meal, even if they don't quite fit into your circle of friends.
- It means meeting for coffee with a struggling young adult or single who needs some encouragement.
- It means reaching out to guests and welcoming them to the family of believers.
- It means Bible Studies in prisons and home visits to the elderly.

Think of someone who attends or used to attend your church. If they were asked if you were a kind person, what would they say? If asked whether you helped them feel welcomed and included within the body of believers, what would be their reply? Let's dig in a little deeper. What kind of church could we have if each of us became mindful of others? What if we made a point to reach out to those beyond our circle?

Don't wait for someone else to extend an invitation to their table. We cannot allow the worldly culture of cliques and exclusionary behaviors to be an acceptable part of God's church. The bottom line is simply this: There is room at Jesus's table, so we have no excuse. We need to make room at ours.

4

THE COMPARISON CONUNDRUM

My mother had a way of keeping me humble. One of her nuggets of wisdom was, "There's always going to be someone better than you. So, it doesn't do you any good to be jealous." She watched me struggle with comparing myself to other girls in the church. She consoled me when I didn't make the Bible College chorale two years in a row. She helped me overcome rejection and feelings of self-loathing. And she kept coming back to these words of wisdom.

As I grew up, my mother's words irked me. *Why can't I be the best at something? When is it my turn to shine?* I would think these thoughts too often for my good. I tried hard not to be jealous. I studied enough of the Bible to understand that jealousy and comparisons displeased God. As the years went on, I made sure I smiled at those who got the solos, speaking engagements, or better book deals, and I prayed that God would bless them in their endeavors. But I kept coming back to the thought: *Why not me? When will it be my turn?*

Worldly culture promotes the ideology of stepping on others to get ahead. That it's perfectly acceptable to plow through those in your way. The world's mentality feeds jealousy and comparison. If we're being honest, the church struggles with it too. I know because I grew up in church, and it was a constant battle in my life, as well as with my church friends.

I was flawed in my thinking, and it was holding me back from everything God had for *me*. His gifts and callings are without repentance, but they will never be fulfilled if we use others' gifts and callings as the measuring stick. When I repented and truly sought the Lord to free me from this toxic thinking, he showed me a powerful truth: Jealousy leads to spiritual destruction, and it keeps us from moving forward in the path God has for us.

The Sin of Jealousy

King Saul had a problem. He couldn't let go of his

jealousy toward David. He literally went mad trying to kill his competition.

> *And it came to pass as they came, when David was returned from the slaughter of the Philistine, that the women came out of all cities of Israel, singing and dancing, to meet king Saul, with tabrets, with joy, and with instruments of musick. And the women answered one another as they played, and said, Saul hath slain his thousands, and David his ten thousands.* **And Saul was very wroth, and the saying displeased him; and he said, They have ascribed unto David ten thousands, and to me they have ascribed but thousands: and what can he have more but the kingdom?** (1 Samuel 18:6-8; *emphasis mine*)

Even though the Bible documents King Saul's jealousy in 1 Samuel 18, the seeds of it had already been planted in his heart. Think about it. In 1 Samuel 15, Samuel rebukes King Saul for his disobedience to God and tells him that the kingdom has been taken from him and given to a neighbor. How many of us would be okay with that? I'd probably be begging and pleading for another chance. It would be hard not to wonder who the "neighbor" was and what they had that I didn't. And in 1 Samuel 17, David is the only one who volunteers to face Goliath, and he defeats the giant. To make matters worse for King Saul, David was the only musician who could soothe the king's nerves and calm the madness. King Saul became consumed. The jealousy ate away at his sanity. It is quite the cautionary tale, yet many in today's church have fallen into a similar comparison conundrum.

So, why exactly is jealousy a sin? Jealousy is an operation of our flesh. In 1 Corinthians 3:3, Paul writes to the believers in Corinth: "For ye are yet carnal: for whereas there is among you envying, and strife, and divisions, are ye not carnal, and walk as men?" The proof was in the pudding. According to Paul, we are carnally minded when we are jealous and stirring up strife. And in Romans 8:7, Paul states that the carnal mind is enmity against God.

Jealousy is a dangerous spiritual path. In Genesis 4, Cain became jealous of his brother, Abel, and he murdered him because of it. In Genesis 37, Joseph's older brothers threw him into a pit to kill him, eventually selling him as a slave and lying to their father. In today's modern culture, jealousy leads to bitterness and a lack of gratitude toward the blessings of God. Jealousy makes us discontent, which does not make us Godly (1 Timothy 6:6).

The Stronghold of Comparison

It is hard to break free from the stronghold of comparison when we are focused on the wrong things. The biblical accounts of King Saul, Cain, and Joseph's older brothers illustrate how the stronghold of comparison leads to rash, sinful actions and the negative consequences of that result.

What does this stronghold look like in our lives?

- Feeling inferior
- Hating someone we see as competition
- Excluding those who don't fit in with us
- Being intimidated by the talents of someone else and measuring it against ourselves
- Becoming jealous and letting that jealousy feed our fears and insecurities

Biblical Warnings

The root of jealousy is comparison, and the Bible is clear that we are to avoid it at all costs.

- "For do I now persuade men, or God? or do I seek to please men? for if I yet pleased men, I should not be the servant of Christ" (Galatians 1:10).

- "But let every man prove his own work, and then shall he have rejoicing in himself alone, and not in another. For every man shall bear his own burden" (Galatians 6:4-5).
- "For **we dare not** make ourselves of the number, or **compare ourselves** with some that commend themselves: but they measuring themselves by themselves, and **comparing themselves among themselves, are not wise**" (2 Corinthians 10:12; **emphasis mine**).
- "Having then gifts differing according to the grace that is given to us, whether prophecy, let us prophesy according to the proportion of faith," (Romans 12:6).
- "For wrath killeth the foolish man, and envy slayeth the silly one" (Job 5:2).
- "But if ye have bitter envying and strife in your hearts, glory not, and lie not against the truth. This wisdom descendeth not from above, but is earthly, sensual, devilish. For where envying and strife is,

there is confusion and every evil work" (James 3:14-16).

- When we compare ourselves to others, it can lead to discontentment. "Not that I speak in respect of want: for I have learned, in **whatsoever state I am, therewith to be content.** I know both how to be abased, and I know how to abound: every where and in all things I am instructed both to be full and to be hungry, both to abound and to suffer need. I can do all things through Christ which strengtheneth me" (Philippians 4:11-13; **emphasis mine**).
- "...That ye might learn in us not to think of men above that which is written, that **no one of you be puffed up** for one against another. **For who maketh thee to differ from another?** and what hast thou that thou didst not receive? now if thou didst receive it, why dost thou glory, as if thou hadst not received it?" (1 Corinthians 4:6-7; **emphasis mine**).
- "Wherefore laying aside all malice, and all guile, and hypocrisies, and **envies,** and all

evil speakings" (1 Peter 2:1; ***emphasis mine***).

These Biblical warnings indicate that jealousy goes against the will of God for our lives. The simple fact is that God loves each of us and, through his grace, gifts us with talents and purpose aligned with his plan for us.

Final Thoughts

In our churches, there are many talents. Each of us has a divine purpose for our lives. That means that someone else's talent is for *their* divine purpose, not ours. So, why compare? Instead, seek God to help you grow in yours. The Bible encourages us that whatever we do, to do it with all our might (Ecclesiastes 9:10).

Fight the carnal thoughts of comparison and jealousy. Lay them at the foot of the cross. Pray for those who have giftings different than you and ask God to bless them for the betterment of God's kingdom. Together, we can use our talents to fulfill the will of God in each of us and in the body of believers. That's what God requires for his church.

5

IDOLATRY

God comes first. It is the first commandment given to Moses, and Jesus repeats the sentiment by explaining that the first commandment is to love God with everything we have. Yet, idolatry has crept into the church and taken residence in many of our lives.

My parents came to the Lord in 1973. My mother was working at a grocery store when one of her friends from work asked her to attend a church service with her for moral support. That invitation changed everything. My mother told my father about the church, and the next Sunday, both of them received the Holy Ghost and were baptized in the precious name of Jesus. That was a year before I was born. I have had the privilege of attending church for my entire life.

When the church doors were open, our family was there. Often, church would take up several days in a week, but it didn't matter to my parents. They had found the truth, and they wanted all that God had for them.

For me, church became old hat. Don't get me wrong, I loved church. I enjoyed the singing and praise. I enjoyed the children's camps and youth retreats. But as I became a teenager, some of it became drudgery. I grew up experiencing the presence of God so often that I became bored with it (we'll talk about apathy in the next chapter). As a teen, I looked to the world for the excitement and novelty that my flesh craved. These desires became idols for me, and they took me down the wrong path.

Idolatry doesn't look the same as it did over 2,000 years ago. In Biblical times, pagan worship was prevalent. God did not tolerate it then, and he doesn't tolerate it now.

> *And when the people saw that Moses delayed to come down out of the mount, the people gathered themselves together unto Aaron, and said unto him, Up, make us gods, which shall go before us; for as for this Moses, the man that brought us up out of the land of Egypt, we wot not what is become of him. And Aaron said unto them,*

*Break off the golden earrings, which are in the ears of your wives, of your sons, and of your daughters, and bring them unto me. And all the people brake off the golden earrings which were in their ears, and brought them unto Aaron. And he received them at their hand, and fashioned it with a graving tool, after he had made it a molten calf: and they said, These be thy gods, O Israel, which brought thee up out of the land of Egypt. And when Aaron saw it, he built an altar before it; and Aaron made proclamation, and said, To morrow is a feast to the Lord. And they rose up early on the morrow, and offered burnt offerings, and brought peace offerings; and the people sat down to eat and to drink, and rose up to play. And the Lord said unto Moses, Go, get thee down; for thy people, which thou broughtest out of the land of Egypt, have corrupted themselves: They have turned aside quickly out of the way which I commanded them: they have made them a molten calf, and have worshipped it, and have sacrificed thereunto, and said, These be thy gods, O Israel, which have brought thee up out of the land of Egypt. And the Lord said unto Moses, **I have seen this people, and, behold, it is a stiffnecked people: Now therefore let me alone, that my wrath may wax hot against them, and that I may consume them: and I will make of thee a great nation.*** (Exodus 32:1-10; **emphasis mine**)

The children of Israel had been through a lot as documented in Exodus. They were slaves in Egypt before God delivered them. They experienced the plagues, watched as God protected them from the angel of death, and literally walked through a parted Red Sea. Even with God's goodness on full display, it didn't take long for them to long for Egypt and forget God's provisions and deliverance.

Modern day idolatry looks a little different than in Biblical days, but the outcome is the same. It angers God. The traditional sense of the word simply means worshipping or bowing to a statue or object connected to some deity, but it also refers to a spiritual heart condition where we place things or people before God. With the children of Israel, their hearts were turned away from God before the golden calf was ever created.

In the New Testament, Paul further explained idolatry when writing to the saints of Colosse. He writes that it is more than bowing to a graven image; it is desiring anything more than God. When we put anything before God, we are participating in idolatry. The end result, just like with the children of Israel, is God's wrath.

The Sin of Idolatry

Most of us don't have graven images that we bow to and worship. We are not in danger of melting all of our gold and building a calf. But we were created to worship, and in today's culture, worshipping our flesh or the momentary pleasures of this world come first. As stated in an earlier chapter, Jesus warned the crowd in Matthew 6 that we serve one master, and there are only two to choose from. If we're not serving God with everything we have, then we are serving our flesh. This is idolatry. Doing so, puts us in enmity against God and reaps a host of negative consequences.

So, if idolatry is more than worshipping graven images, what is it, and how is it sin? In Colossians, Paul states that covetousness is idolatry. When we desire what others have and are envious of the lives they live, we are practicing idolatry.

In 1 Samuel 15, Samuel rebukes Saul and provides another example of idolatry: "For rebellion is as the sin of witchcraft, and ***stubbornness is as iniquity and idolatry***. Because thou hast rejected the word of the Lord, he hath also rejected thee from being king" (1 Samuel 15:23; ***emphasis mine).*** From King Saul's example, we see that refusing to submit to God and his Word is rebellion and idolatry.

In today's culture, our refusal to submit to the Word of God is partly because we have learned to worship ourselves. We have become our own god. This manifests through pride, vain ambition, jealousy, and selfishness. This form of idolatry demands: "What are you doing for me?" or "How does this benefit me?" or "If I don't want to do something, I'm not going to do it." The world views these sentiments as drawing boundaries or protecting ourselves from manipulation, but these sentiments are also reflective of a selfish, self-serving attitude that permeates our culture. This attitude devalues our relationships with other people because we are too busy trying to make ourselves happy.

Loving God, according to Scripture, is keeping His commandments, worshiping Him in Spirit and in truth, offering thanksgiving for all He has done for us, and abiding in Him. Our relationship with Jesus matters more than anything else. This is a *daily* walk with God. It is pursuing him first and refusing to allow anything or anyone to come before him. When we detour from this, it is a sin.

Idolatry's Stronghold

It is hard to imagine that today's church struggles with idolatry. But the thing about strongholds is that they don't happen overnight. For example, a person came to the Lord and fell in love with him, committing their lives to serving Jesus. As time passes, they fell into some habits that took them away from daily devotion. Soon, they started to skip a service or two for different reasons, like a sporting event, or even laundry. This person still believed in Jesus and still loved him...to an extent. From this point, worldly habits and behavior started trickling in again. God is no longer first in this person's life, and the stronghold of idolatry has taken his place.

Here are some examples of what idolatry's stronghold may look like in each of us:

- Refusing to submit to God's Word
- Being envious and covetous of other people and their possessions/talents
- Our personal ambition (we put our goals and dreams before our relationship with God)
- Materialism (we desire things more than God's presence)

- Entertainment addiction (gaming, sports, social media, streaming platforms, movies; our lust for entertainment comes before God)
- Becoming our own god (self-love and self-promotion, where it's less about Jesus and more about us)
- Worshipping nature and reverencing the universe (the sun, the moon, the stars)
- Anything or anyone that comes before our relationship with God.

The Bible repeatedly calls God "jealous." God is holy, righteous, and perfect, so this jealousy refers to his passion and desire for an intimate relationship with us. The stronghold of idolatry is as if we're thumbing our nose at God and telling him that we'll get to him when/if we get a chance.

Biblical Warnings

The first commandment God established with Moses for his people was that God came first and nothing was to take his place. Even before Moses, God sought the hearts of man, testing Abraham's commitment to him. In Genesis 22, God directed Abraham to take his son, Isaac, and offer him as a sacrifice. Verses 11 and 12 explain why:

And the angel of the Lord called unto him out of heaven, and said, Abraham, Abraham: and he said, Here am I. And he said, Lay not thine hand upon the lad, neither do thou any thing unto him: **for now I know that thou fearest God, seeing thou hast not withheld thy son, thine only son from me.** *(emphasis mine)*

It matters to God who we worship. It matters to him whether he is truly Lord of our lives.

- "Who changed the truth of God into a lie, **and worshipped and served the creature more than the Creator**, who is blessed for ever. Amen" (Romans 1:25; **emphasis mine).**
- "Mortify therefore your members which are upon the earth; fornication, uncleanness, inordinate affection, evil concupiscence, **and covetousness, which is idolatry**: For which things' sake **the wrath of God** cometh on the children of disobedience:" (Colossians 3:5-6; **emphasis mine).**

- **"Their sorrows shall be multiplied that hasten after another god**: their drink offerings of blood will I not offer, nor take up their names into my lips" (Psalms 16:4; *emphasis mine)*.
- "Thou shalt have no other gods before me" (Exodus 20:3).
- "Little children, keep yourselves from idols. Amen" (1 John 5:21).
- "They that observe lying vanities *(worthless idols)* forsake their own mercy" (Jonah 2:8; *clarification mine)*.
- "Turn ye not unto idols, nor make to yourselves molten gods: I am the Lord your God" (Leviticus 19:4).
- "Wherefore, my dearly beloved, flee from idolatry" (1 Corinthians 10:14).

Final Thoughts

In many ways, we are too busy enjoying life and pursuing our dreams to truly put God first. We are blessed and prosperous, and just like with the 10 lepers who were healed in Luke 17, where only one returned to Jesus to thank him, we're too busy enjoying our blessings to give God the worship and reverence that are his and his alone.

When writing this chapter, I asked myself these thought-provoking questions:

1. Do I pursue God daily? How would I describe my relationship with him?
2. Do my children reverence God? Do I incorporate devotion and prayer in their daily lives?
3. Does my family put the things of God first? Do my children know from my example that nothing comes before God in our home?

When we chose Christ and applied his name to our lives through water baptism, we became a part of God's people. Our covenant with God means that we have left our past lives and are now "joint-heirs with Christ" (Romans 8:17). And what a blessing this is for us! As Paul says in 1 Thessalonians 1:9-10:

*For they themselves shew of us what manner of entering in we had unto you, and **how ye turned to God from idols to serve the living and true God**; And to wait for his Son from heaven, whom he raised from the dead,* *even Jesus, which delivered us from the wrath to come.* ***(emphasis mine)***

Let the church proclaim it to the world and live it every day: We serve the one true God! And what an honor and privilege it is.

6

APATHY

Weddings are often beautiful events where a man and woman vow to love and cherish each other for the rest of their lives. Most of us cherish these moments and enjoy celebrating as couples make this commitment before God.

It doesn't take long—maybe a year or two—before reality sets in, and we realize that marriage comes with challenges. Our hearts may no longer pound in excitement at the thought of time spent with them. Many of us no longer feel butterflies at the very sight of our spouse. We may prefer time alone rather than time spent with each other. We may lean on others for friendship and solidarity because we find it easier than developing friendship and solidarity with our spouses. The wedding day is long forgotten, and without an attitude shift, we're just plodding through life with someone we merely tolerate. If we're not careful, as the years march forth, we may pull away from our spouse and simply become apathetic in our relationship.

There is a saying that familiarity breeds contempt. Let's change this a bit: familiarity breeds apathy. This can be true in our relationships with each other, and unfortunately, it can be true in our relationship with God. Think about when we first fell in love with Jesus. The peace and joy we found in him overwhelmed us. We jumped at the chance to be at church when the doors opened. Special services...we were there. Prayer meetings...we were there. Charity work in the community...we were there. Loving God was easy. So, what's the problem?

Just like in our relationships with each other, without a conscientious pursuit of our Savior, we will drift apart from Jesus. This will be our choice, not his. It doesn't happen overnight, but apathy in the body of believers is a real struggle in today's church.

- In the past 25 years, church attendance has consistently declined.[1]

- Even though over 70% of Americans say they believe in God, approximately 20% of them attend church on a regular basis.
- Thousands of church doors have closed for good.
- Of those who say they are Christian, 60% say they attend church once or twice a month.
- Only 30% of Christians say they have a high-level of involvement in their church.[2]
- In a recent survey, 75% of Protestant pastors admitted that apathy was the biggest challenge in their congregations, referring to a lack of commitment and involvement.[3]

Why is this? An earlier chapter shared how little we truly know of God's Word. If we're not pursuing God, then we are more apt to operate in our flesh and become apathetic to the things of God. Our devotion to God wanes, and we allow busyness and the cares of this life to come between our relationship with him.

Worldly culture tells us that it's acceptable to place God on a shelf while we live our day-to-day lives. It says that there is nothing wrong with skipping church for a round of golf or our child's sporting event. It justifies our distractions by saying that we can still love God and focus on our needs. The world's culture pats us on the head and says that Jesus is okay with us living a life where he is not a part of it.

To be more specific, apathy is more than not caring. It is disinterest, indifference, or lacking purpose and/or motivation. When someone is apathetic, they detach themselves from relationships and situations that are too involved. The statistics in the earlier paragraphs alarmingly show that most U.S. citizens are apathetic in their religious service attendance, and even those who are more regular church attendees do not serve the church in any significant way.

In many cases, we say we love God, but we love ourselves more. We enjoy what we feel at church, but it stops there. Our lives aren't changed, we've lost the reverence we once had for our Savior, and we live among the world as part of their culture. We say we're Christians, but our hearts and our lifestyles say otherwise.

The Sin of Apathy

Apathy is dangerous for us because it's indifference to the things of God and a disinterest in our relationship with him. Some suggest that apathy is the opposite of love because with apathy, we no longer care about the other person or what happens in other's lives. When we lose this love, we become apathetic. This becomes sin.

In Revelation, Jesus reprimands the church in Ephesus for losing their first love.

> *Nevertheless **I have somewhat against thee, because thou hast left thy first love.** Remember therefore from whence thou art fallen, and repent, and do the first works; or else I will come unto thee quickly, and will remove thy candlestick out of his place, except thou repent.* (Revelation 2:4-5; **emphasis mine**)

What is their first love? It is what ours should be: loving God with everything in us. How do we effectively do that? Our relationship to Jesus is compared to a bride and her groom. The church is the bride of Christ, and the Bible says that Jesus is coming back for a bride without spot or blemish.

When we are born again, the miraculous happens. We begin a covenant with God. If you study the Old Testament, you will find God desiring a people who are chosen and called out from the world. When we repent of our sins and are baptized in Jesus' name, we are taking on his name. This action of obedience separates us from the world and joins us in a covenant with our Savior.

There are two crucial components to this: waiting for him and preparing for him. In Jesus' parable about the wedding feast, everyone was too busy to come to the celebration. And in the parable of the ten virgins, only half of them were fully prepared for his entrance. All of this—both the waiting and the preparing—require action. According to these Biblical examples, apathy then leads to separation from God.

The Stronghold of Apathy

The stronghold of apathy starts with busyness, distractions, boredom, or disappointment. Soon, we make excuses for why God is not a priority. It begins with justifying our thoughts and actions even though they are contrary to the Word. We might say things like, "What's the big deal? It's not like the church needs me." We might hit the snooze button one too many times and then rush to get the day started. We might allow the routine of church and devotion to become lackluster and ritualistic. "But hey," we might say to justify our busyness or list of reasons why our relationship with God is taking a back seat, "At least I still listen to the Christian music station." What does becoming spiritually apathetic look like?

- It is giving in to distractions.
- It is being too busy to develop and deepen our relationship with God.
- It is not desiring the things of God.
- It is loving the world and the things of the world.
- It is a lack of commitment to serving the church and people of God.

Apathy doesn't need an invitation into our lives to make camp and stick around. It shows up, pitches its tent, and puts up its feet. Sometimes, our lives become so hectic that we don't even realize that we've stopped praying and reading the Bible. With the stronghold of apathy, our spiritual lives are stuck in a rut.

Biblical Warnings

Jesus had harsh words for apathy. In Matthew 7:21-23, he warns:

*Not every one that saith unto me, Lord, Lord, shall enter into the kingdom of heaven; but he that doeth the will of my Father which is in heaven. Many will say to me in that day, Lord, Lord, have we not prophesied in thy name? and in thy name have cast out devils? and in thy name done many wonderful works? And then will **I profess unto them, I never knew you:** depart from me, ye that work iniquity.*

From this example, we learn that lip service and empty actions do not move the heart of God. He is looking for a relationship. Knowing him refers to an intimate, close bond like we have in a marriage contract. If our walk with God has become stagnant, if other things have taken priority over our service to him, if we have lost interest in pursuing him, then we have erred. The Word declares it:

- "He that loveth not **knoweth not God**; for God is love" (1 John 4:8; **emphasis mine**).
- "So then because **thou art lukewarm**, and neither cold nor hot, **I will spue thee out of my mouth**" (Revelation 3:16; **emphasis mine**).
- "**Not slothful in business**, fervent in spirit **(not being apathetic),** serving the Lord"

(Romans 12:11; **emphasis and clarification mine**)
- "And it shall come to pass at that time, that I will search Jerusalem with candles, and punish the men that are settled on their lees: that say in their heart, The Lord will not do good, neither will he do evil" (Zephaniah 1:12).
- "And because iniquity shall abound, **the love of many shall wax cold**. But he that shall endure unto the end, the same shall be saved" (Matthew 24:12-13; **emphasis mine**).
- "Therefore we ought to give the more earnest heed to the things which we have heard, **lest at any time we should let them slip**. For if the word spoken by angels was stedfast, and every transgression and disobedience received a just recompence of reward; **How shall we escape, if we neglect so great salvation**; which at the first began to be spoken by the Lord, and was confirmed unto us by them that heard him; God also bearing them witness, both with signs and wonders, and with divers miracles, and gifts of the Holy Ghost,

according to his own will?" (Hebrews 2:1-4; *emphasis mine*).
- "Be watchful, and strengthen the things which remain, that are ready to die: for I have not found thy works perfect before God" (Revelation 3:2).
- "Having the understanding darkened, ***being alienated from the life of God through the ignorance that is in them***, because of the blindness of their heart: ***Who being past feeling*** have given themselves over unto lasciviousness, to work all uncleanness with greediness" (Ephesians 4:18-19; *emphasis mine*).
- "Son of man, thou dwellest in the midst of a rebellious house, ***which have eyes to see, and see not***; ***they have ears to hear, and hear not***: for they are a rebellious house" (Ezekiel 12:2; *emphasis mine*).
- "Therefore to him that knoweth to do good, and doeth it not, ***to him it is sin***" (James 4:17; *emphasis mine*).

The Bible is the infallible, unshakable, never-changing Word of God. When the church stays rooted and devoted to Scripture, apathy will have no place in our hearts. It will have to leave.

Final Thoughts

We can attend church services and still be apathetic. We can sing and shout at the altar, and then go home and not say two words to God. We can enjoy the company of the brethren yet turn a cold shoulder to our neighbors or co-workers. We can pursue our desires at the expense of others and go on about life like it's no big deal. We can praise God with our lips yet become indifferent toward him in our hearts.

Be careful of apathy. It's a sneaky sin. It distracts us with the cares of life and the pursuit of pleasure, so much so that our love for God grows cold.

The necessary solution to overcoming apathy in our hearts and lives is to love God fiercely every single day. And the proof will be in the pudding. It'll be in our daily private devotions with him. It will be in our interactions with people. It will be in our humility and service to the kingdom. Let's shake off the apathy in our hearts and turn to Jesus once more.

7

THE SPIRIT OF OFFENSE

We live in a lawsuit culture. If something goes wrong, then it's someone else's fault. Since the worldly culture not only embraces self-love but also the blame game, we struggle to look within ourselves when we make a mistake.

- If we're late for work, it's the fault of the slow drivers.
- If we hurt someone's feelings, well, that's on them. All we're doing is being honest.
- If we have a negative balance in our bank account, it's the fault of businesses for depositing the payment too soon or the bank for not giving us a few extra days.

- If we can't pay our bills, it's the fault of our employers for not paying us enough or the government for taking too much out of our checks.

This mentality finds its way into the church.

- If we don't get a solo, then we'll pout and talk bad about the person who did.
- If we don't get recognized, we'll go somewhere else where we will be recognized.
- If the church leadership doesn't comply with our demands, then they are trying to hold us back.

This blame game breeds offense, and many in society and in the church walk around with chips on their shoulders. When someone is in a constant state of offense, they point a finger at others, placing the blame upon anyone but themselves. The spirit of offense is contrary to the will of God. It blinds us to truth and justifies faulty thinking. It causes spiritual destruction, it's dysfunctional, and it has no place in the body of believers.

The Sin of Offense

Each of us has struggled with minor irritations or annoyances. It is the way of life. The challenge comes when we don't let go of the frustrations that arise from these events. If we're not careful, these minor annoyances can fester and grow into anger, bitterness, and unforgiveness. These negative emotions are the symptoms of offense. When offended, we often feel insulted, and that insult eats away at us. With offense, we make hasty decisions. We are quick to retaliate. We build a wall of unforgiveness between us and those who offended us. In each of these situations, we are behaving in a way that is the opposite of what Jesus would do.

While dying on the cross, Jesus prayed that God would forgive them—the very people who beat him and crucified him—because they did not fully understand what they were doing. His love kept him on that cross. When Jesus was resurrected and appeared before Peter, he didn't accuse or condemn him. He didn't remind him of his failings. Jesus wasn't offended that his disciples all scattered during the crucifixion, and because Jesus forgave and took the high road, many lives were and are forever changed.

Being offended is a sign of pride and an unforgiving heart. Jesus shared the parable of the unforgiving servant in Matthew 18:23-35:

> *Therefore is the kingdom of heaven likened unto a certain king, which would take account of his servants. And when he had begun to reckon, one was brought unto him, which owed him ten thousand talents. But forasmuch as he had not to pay, his lord commanded him to be sold, and his wife, and children, and all that he had, and payment to be made. The servant therefore fell down, and worshipped him, saying, Lord, have patience with me, and I will pay thee all. Then the lord of that servant was moved with compassion, and loosed him, and forgave him the debt. But the same servant went out, and found one of his fellowservants, which owed him an hundred pence: and he laid hands on him, and took him by the throat, saying, Pay me that thou owest. And his fellowservant fell down at his feet, and besought him, saying, Have patience with me, and I will pay thee all. And he would not: but went and cast him into prison, till he should pay the debt. So when his fellowservants saw what was done, they were very sorry, and came and told unto their lord all that was done. Then his lord, after that he had called him, said unto him, O thou wicked servant, I forgave thee all that debt, because thou desiredst me: Shouldest not thou*

also have had compassion on thy fellowservant, even as I had pity on thee? And his lord was wroth, and delivered him to the tormentors, till he should pay all that was due unto him. ***So likewise shall my heavenly Father do also unto you, if ye from your hearts forgive not every one his brother their trespasses.*** ***(emphasis mine)***

What a powerful warning about holding onto offense. Our Heavenly Father could hold onto offense if he so desired. Each of us would be guilty, deserving eternal damnation. Thankfully, he is compassionate and longsuffering, "...not willing that any should perish, but that all should come to repentance" (2 Peter 3:9). When we hold onto offense, we are rebelling against the Word of God. This is sin and, if not rectified, could keep us from heaven.

The Stronghold of Offense

The stronghold of offense hurts the offended more than the offender. It stifles the fruit of the spirit in one's life and instead grows bitterness and other negative attributes within us. It can also create a *victim mentality* within the individual. Victims feel that events happen *to* them, not *because of* them. It's easier to blame someone else than to look at ourselves and make adjustments.

In worldly culture, holding a grudge means protecting oneself from hurt or insult. Some argue that it's building walls around our hearts to protect us from mistreatment. Boundaries are fine, but the Bible says that we should not hold onto offense or allow hurt feelings to grow. Jesus admonishes us to go directly to the person who wronged us:

> *Moreover if thy brother shall trespass against thee, go and tell him his fault between thee and him alone: if he shall hear thee, thou hast gained thy brother. (Matthew 18:15)*

Later, in the same chapter, Peter approaches Jesus and seeks clarification:

> *Then came Peter to him, and said, Lord, how oft shall my brother sin against me, and I forgive him? till seven times? Jesus saith unto him, I say not unto thee, Until seven times: but, Until seventy times seven. (Matthew 18:21-22)*

The stronghold of offense then takes hold when we choose to not forgive those who hurt or insulted us. It isn't only prominent in worldly culture; this stronghold plagues many of us in church circles. We perceive someone has wronged us, and we let that fester until it consumes us. What does the stronghold of offense look like in the life of a believer?

- It looks like not responding well to criticism.
- It looks like gossiping about and undermining others with whom you disagree.
- It looks like harboring resentment toward someone we feel has wronged us.
- It looks like bitterness toward Godly leadership for daring to align us to Scripture.
- It looks like unforgiveness and a refusal to let go of the past.

The Pharisees and religious leaders of Jesus' time were offended at Jesus. They didn't like his command of crowds or the miracles he'd perform for those less fortunate. They became furious when Jesus forgave the woman caught in adultery, and they struggled with his authority. How could this son of a carpenter from Nazareth dare forgive someone as if he was God?

Their offense grew to the point that they were consumed with a desire for retaliation, ultimately releasing a criminal back into society so they could crucify Jesus instead. God help the church break free from the stronghold of offense before it creates chaos and destruction to the family of God.

Biblical Warnings

The Word of God warns us that offense has no place in the body of believers and that it is like a prison to those consumed by it.

- "A brother offended is harder to be won than a strong city: and their contentions are like the bars of a castle" (Proverbs 18:19).
- "For where envying and strife is, *there is confusion and every evil work*," (James 3:16; *emphasis mine*).
- "He that covereth a transgression seeketh love; but *he that repeateth a matter separateth very friends*" (Proverbs 17:9; *emphasis mine*).
- "Brethren, if a man be overtaken in a fault, ye which are spiritual, restore such an one

in the spirit of meekness; considering thyself, lest thou also be tempted. Bear ye one another's burdens, and so fulfil the law of Christ. ***For if a man think himself to be something, when he is nothing, he deceiveth himself***" (Galatians 6:1-3; ***emphasis mine***).

Instead of offense, the Bible requires love and forgiveness.

- "Thou shalt not avenge, nor bear any grudge against the children of thy people, but thou shalt love thy neighbour as thyself: I am the Lord" (Leviticus 19:18).
- "Forbearing one another, and forgiving one another, if any man have a quarrel against any: even as Christ forgave you, so also do ye" (Colossians 3:13).
- "Take heed to yourselves: If thy brother trespass against thee, rebuke him; and if he repent, forgive him. And if he trespass against thee seven times in a day, and seven times in a day turn again to thee, saying, I repent; thou shalt forgive him" (Luke 17:3-4).

The Spirit of Offense is embraced in the world's culture, but according to Scripture, it is a forgiving spirit that truly sets us free.

Final Thoughts

People are imperfect, and we make mistakes often. The church, too, is full of imperfect people trying to serve a perfect God. For the church to thrive and be in unity, we must not allow the spirit of offense to take hold of us.

Holding onto negative feelings only imprisons us. It is impossible to harbor the spirit of offense, and at the same time, love others. The world's culture may justify holding a grudge or vowing revenge, but that is not God's way.

If Jesus can forgive us, do we not owe it to each other to offer grace and forgiveness? Let the church say "amen."

8

THE CRITICAL SPIRIT

Part of my career is editing others' manuscripts, and constructive criticism is part of the process. The goal is to make their writing shine. To accomplish this, the writer will take my edits and apply them to their manuscript.

In much the same way, there are times when we are offered constructive criticism so that we may change direction or shift our perspective to make wise decisions. Constructive criticism is meant to help, and the spirit behind it is one of encouragement and growth. This is not to be confused with having a critical spirit. One is needed in the church, but the other attacks the church.

Over twenty years ago I wrote a church drama for Easter. The church got involved, and we started weekly practices. All was going well, or so I thought, until I walked into the church kitchen to drop off a snack. As I entered, I overheard three women talking about what a mess the drama was, and how I had no idea what I was doing. The words were harsh and critical. They spotted me before I could turn around, and I remember vividly how embarrassed I was that they caught me hearing their conversation. Two of them seemed to be just as embarrassed as I was and apologized quickly. The other one held her head high, shrugged her shoulders, and said, "Well, it's true."

A critical spirit is a complaining spirit. Its purpose is to grumble and tear down a person, group, or idea. With a critical spirit, the goal is not to necessarily fix anything but to simply murmur and gossip about it to anyone willing to listen. A critical spirit is in direct opposition to a grateful heart and optimistic outlook. And if the enemy can sow seeds of discord in the church, then the church will never reach the unity needed for major revival.

The children of Israel were guilty of grumbling and complaining. They were quick to forget the provisions and blessings of God and would complain about a variety of issues. They complained they had no water, they complained they had no food, and then they complained that they didn't like the food. There seemed to be no pleasing these people!

> *And Moses said, This shall be, when the Lord shall give you in the evening flesh to eat, and in the morning bread to the full; for that the Lord heareth your murmurings which ye murmur against him: and what are we? your murmurings are not against us, but against the Lord.* (Exodus 16:8)

God was not amused. In one instance, he allowed snakes into their tents, and many died. In another example, he opened the ground up and swallowed the complaining parties. To put it mildly, God doesn't appreciate or tolerate a critical spirit.

The Sin of the Critical Spirit

Life is full of ups and downs because we live in a fallen world. How we deal with life's challenges defines who we are and whether we identify with the world's culture or God's kingdom culture. When we approach challenges with anger, bitterness, and/or complaints, instead of trusting in God and behaving in a way that pleases him, we become out of alignment with the will of God and are operating in our flesh.

With a critical spirit, we easily find fault and struggle to control our tongue or emotions. We begin to walk around with a chip on our shoulder, and we become difficult to please or pacify. No one is safe from our biting words, even though most of the negative remarks are behind the person's back. Someone with a critical spirit approaches God in the same way. We struggle with feeling grateful for a blessing, and instead we start grumbling about something else that God hasn't answered yet.

When we harbor a critical spirit, we are outside of the will of God, which is sin. We can't have a critical spirit and have the mind of Christ. We can't have a critical spirit and love others. We can't have a critical spirit and walk in faith and gratitude.

The Stronghold of a Critical Spirit

The stronghold of being critical starts with our outlook. How do we handle life's difficulties? How do we react when others don't agree with us? How do we handle situations outside our control that are not going our way? Answers to these questions will give us a better understanding of our overall outlook. If we automatically assume the worst, if we tend to approach life with a glass half empty mindset, then we may have the stronghold of a critical spirit.

There are several ways this stronghold manifests in our lives.

- The critical spirit chooses to complain instead of being part of the solution.
- The critical spirit gossips about someone to others instead of praying for them or supporting them on their spiritual journey.
- The critical spirit holds a grudge or offense instead of approaching the person and having an honest, gracious conversation.
- The critical spirit shares our opinion freely without request and shuts down any conversation that could be perceived as different than ours.
- The critical spirit is quick to react in anger or frustration and quick to grumble.

The stronghold of a critical spirit creates discord among the body of believers. It angers God, and according to Scripture, we will have to face the consequences for such negativity.

Biblical Warnings

The Bible illustrates how complaining angers God. In Numbers 11, the children of Israel brought punishment upon themselves:

> *And when the people complained, it displeased the Lord: and the Lord heard it; and his anger was kindled; and the fire of the Lord burnt among them, and consumed them that were in the uttermost parts of the camp. And the people cried unto Moses; and when Moses prayed unto the Lord, the fire was quenched.* (Numbers 11:1-2)

One would think that the children of Israel would learn their lesson, but several chapters later, they were complaining again:

> *And they journeyed from mount Hor by the way of the Red sea, to compass the land of Edom: and the soul of the people was much discouraged because of the way. And* **the people spake against God**, *and against Moses, Wherefore have ye brought us up out of Egypt to die in the wilderness? for there is no bread, neither is there any water; and our soul loatheth this light bread.* **And the Lord sent fiery serpents among the people, and they**

bit the people; and much people of Israel died. (Numbers 21:4-6; ***emphasis mine***)

These examples show an ungrateful nation who often forgot the goodness of the Lord. Their ungratefulness is evident by their griping. And God was having none of it.

If we think we're any better, we might want to reconsider. Sometimes we turn a blind eye to God's blessings and instead focus on things, people, and life circumstances that are not going our way. In a worldly culture where our opinion matters most—and everyone else is wrong—we can mistakenly act the same way toward God. But the Bible couldn't be any clearer that we are to turn away from a critical spirit and embrace a grateful heart:

- "***Therefore thou art inexcusable, O man, whosoever thou art that judgest***: for wherein thou judgest another, thou condemnest thyself; for thou that judgest doest the same things. But we are sure that the judgment of God is according to truth against them which commit such things. ***And thinkest thou this, O man, that judgest them which do such things,*** *and doest the same, that thou shalt escape the judgment of God?"* (Romans 2:1-3; **emphasis mine**)

- "Judge not, that ye be not judged. For with what judgment ye judge, ye shall be judged: and with what measure ye mete, it shall be measured to you again. And why beholdest thou the mote that is in thy brother's eye, but considerest not the beam that is in thine own eye? Or how wilt thou say to thy brother, Let me pull out the mote out of thine eye; and, behold, a beam is in thine own eye? ***Thou hypocrite, first cast out the beam out of thine own eye; and then shalt thou see clearly to cast out the mote out of thy brother's eye***" (Matthew 7:1-5; **emphasis mine**).

- "***Speak not evil one of another, brethren***. He that speaketh evil of his brother, and judgeth his brother, speaketh evil of the law, and judgeth the law: but if thou judge the law, thou art not a doer of the law, but a judge" (James 4:11; **emphasis mine**).

- "***Let no corrupt communication proceed out of your mouth***, but that which is good to the use of edifying, that it may minister grace unto the hearers" (Ephesians 4:29; ***emphasis mine***).

- "Grudge not one against another, brethren, ***lest ye be condemned***: behold, the judge standeth before the door" (James 5:9; ***emphasis mine***).
- "Neither murmur ye, as ***some of them also murmured***, and ***were destroyed*** of the destroyer" (1 Corinthians 10:10; ***emphasis mine***).
- "But murmured in their tents, and hearkened not unto the voice of the Lord" (Psalms 106:25).
- "***Do all things without murmurings and disputings***: That ye may be blameless and harmless, the sons of God, without rebuke, in the midst of a crooked and perverse nation, ***among whom ye shine as lights in the world;*** Holding forth the word of life; that I may rejoice in the day of Christ, that I have not run in vain, neither laboured in vain" (Philippians 2:14-16; ***emphasis mine***).
- "Charity suffereth long, and is kind; charity envieth not; charity vaunteth not itself, is not puffed up, Doth not behave

itself unseemly, seeketh not her own, ***is not easily provoked, thinketh no evil;***" (1 Corinthians 13:4-5; ***emphasis mine***).

Let us heed the Word of the Lord and stop being critical before we hurt others, hurt the church, and hurt ourselves.

Final Thoughts

It is easy to fall into murmuring and grumbling. Seeing others err or do something differently than we would do may bother us and incite us to freely give our opinion through gossip or criticism. Sometimes we walk around with a frown or continued offense, and how we treat people becomes a reflection of those negative feelings.

We cannot love others while holding onto a critical spirit. More specifically, we can potentially hurt our brothers and sisters in Christ by harboring negative emotions or constant griping. Think about how powerful the church will be when we overcome a critical spirit and see others as Christ does. What a difference it will make!

9

GLUTTONY

Donuts, cupcakes, cookies, and candy bars. Oh my! Buffets, dessert trays, and second helpings. Oh me!

The pursuit of pleasure is an integral part of worldly culture. "If it feels good, do it," became the mantra for many. Some have joked that in church circles, the mantra became, "If it tastes good, eat it."

Gluttony is many things. It is the pursuit of excess and indulgence, lacking self-control. And in our modern church, it has become an acceptable sin. We'll preach hellfire and brimstone over sexual immorality, and we'll host AA meetings and recovery groups. And all of this is needed. Yet, we do not dare to examine ourselves for this shortcoming of our flesh. Just as some pursue pleasure in other ways, many of us pursue pleasure in our food and delicacies.

As is the case with anything in terms of feeding our flesh—both physical and spiritual—if we're not careful, excessive indulgence becomes the norm. It's intoxicating. It's addicting. And it takes Jesus off the throne of our hearts.

In Romans 12:1, Paul commends us: "I beseech you therefore, brethren, by the mercies of God, that ***ye present your bodies a living sacrifice***, holy, acceptable unto God, which is your reasonable service" **(emphasis mine).** Our church culture promotes the sacrificing of our bodies in many positive, life-affirming ways, but gluttony has become more the norm in our churches than not. Is it holy to overindulge?

It's hard to discuss this because we need food to live. It's not as if we can turn off eating and never pick it up again. Fellowshipping with others over a meal or dessert brings enjoyment in our lives, and there is nothing necessarily wrong with this. Unfortunately, most Americans are addicted to food, specifically sugar. So, every time we eat, if we're not careful, we are feeding our addiction. This is hard to balance, but we must endeavor to create this balance, or food becomes an idol.

This is not pointing a finger at those of us who

struggle with our weight. There are, at times, many other reasons for excess pounds than gluttony. Some gluttons may be rail thin. And there are those who are gluttons, but not in terms of food. They are gluttonous in overindulgences in other areas. However, if we are truly being honest, our food addictions often lead to excess weight and physical ailments. It is hard to hide gluttony because we wear the effects of it daily.

At my heaviest I weighed over 300 pounds. It was no one else's fault. I prayed and prayed. I begged God to take away food cravings and to help me stop having urges to consume whatever was in sight. In all transparency, I even went under the knife for the lap band surgery to help control my cravings. It didn't work. I maybe lost 20 pounds. But I was still addicted to food, especially sugar. My cravings were still powerful. I tried every diet under the sun. Sometimes I would be successful and lose 20 pounds. One time on Weight Watchers, I lost 51 pounds before slowly putting it all back on. It wasn't that I didn't love God. It wasn't that He wasn't first in my life, but I simply couldn't get a handle on my appetite.

My struggle has helped open my eyes to the addictions of others. I may not be addicted to alcohol, pain pills, cigarettes, or drugs, but I am addicted to something that is just as powerful. How can I point a finger at someone just because their addiction is different than mine? And if we do not subject our flesh to the plan of God, we will reap the wages of this sin. The cost of gluttony is death just as with everything else that isn't God in our lives (Romans 6:23).

The Sin of Gluttony or Unsatiable Appetites

Our culture struggles with controlling our appetites. Not only do we lack control of our increased appetite for food, but we also lack control of our appetites for pleasure, for violence, for entertainment, or for self-promotion. This pursuit of instant gratification and pleasure has increased addictions in a variety of areas such as an addiction to media, devices, pornography, sugar, etc. One researcher explained that all of us gravitate to some area of pleasure, and if we're not careful, become addicted to it.[1] Addiction is the manifestation of a lack of self-control.

- Appetite for pleasure
- Appetite for power or fame

- Appetite of self-indulgence
- Appetite for love and acceptance
- Appetite for entertainment

Having an appetite means having a desire or fondness for something. Having an insatiable appetite is wanting as much of something as one can possibly get. But do we have an appetite for the things of God? Do we pursue him and his kingdom more than any other appetite?

The Stronghold of Gluttony

What one item do you enjoy eating or drinking daily? Could you give it up? Could you do it for a week? In Bro. Josh Herring's book, *Fast Forward*, he explains the power and need for fasting in our lives.[2] When I read the book, I realized that I did not fast like I should, and the reasons behind my lack of fasting had to do with my food cravings and food addictions. I was unwilling to give up certain foods. I struggled with even giving up a meal.

Case in point: I love coffee. Every morning, I pour a cup of joe with some creamer, then sit down to read my devotional and have some prayer time. It's routine. I will also stop by the local coffee shop on a consistent basis and indulge in my favorite latte. One time, during a powerful prayer meeting, my pastor's wife asked us to give up something we enjoy for 21 days. The idea was to simply give it to God and then seek His presence. The Spirit whispered, "Give up coffee." I remember that moment because I fought it! I told myself that I would give something else up, but *not* that. But God wasn't done dealing with me. The next morning when I went to pour a cup of coffee, I felt convicted. I heard the Spirit ask, "Can you not give it up for three weeks?" Long story short: I did give it up, and it was the longest three weeks of my life. It was a constant battle with my flesh. I grumbled and complained nearly the entire 21 days. How did this fast glorify God? How did it strengthen my walk with him? Short answer: it didn't. My heart wasn't in the right place because I was too busy grieving what I couldn't have.

Now just because we enjoy a latte every morning doesn't mean we're gluttonous for it. However, the stronghold of gluttony is found in our unwillingness to give up the over-indulgence of food or other overindulgences like media consumption. What does this stronghold look like in our lives?

- Pursuing pleasure or excess over our relationship with God
- Lacking self-control: "I just can't stop."
- Choosing excess or fulfilling our desires over the needs of others
- The inability to give up our source of pleasure or excess for a time of prayer and fasting

Biblical Warnings

The stronghold of gluttony is therefore rooted in idolatry. According to Scripture, the end result is our destruction, both in the spiritual and in the natural.

- "Whose end is destruction, ***whose God is their belly***, and whose glory is in their shame, who mind earthly things" (Philippians 3:19; ***emphasis mine***).
- "Know ye not that ye are the temple of God, and that the Spirit of God dwelleth in you? ***If any man defile the temple of God, him shall God destroy***; for the temple of God is holy, which temple ye are" (1 Corinthians 3:16-17; ***emphasis mine***).

- "And they tempted God in their heart by asking meat for their lust" (Psalms 78:18).
- "And they shall say unto the elders of his city, This our son is stubborn and rebellious, he will not obey our voice; he is a glutton and a drunkard" (Deuteronomy 21:20).
- "For all that is in the world, the lust of the flesh, and the lust of the eyes, and the pride of life, is not of the Father, but is of the world" (1 John 2:16).
- "And take heed to yourselves, lest at any time your hearts be overcharged with surfeiting *(eating in excess),* and drunkenness, and cares of this life, and so that day come upon you unawares" (Luke 21:34; *clarification and emphasis mine*).
- "When thou sittest to eat with a ruler, consider diligently what is before thee: And put a knife to thy throat, if thou be a man given to appetite. Be not desirous of his dainties: for they are deceitful meat" (Proverbs 23:1-3).
- "Ye cannot drink the cup of the Lord, and the cup of devils: ye cannot be partakers of the Lord's table, and of the table of devils.

Do we provoke the Lord to jealousy? are we stronger than he? All things are lawful for me, but all things are not expedient: all things are lawful for me, but all things edify not" (1 Corinthians 10:21-23).
- "Behold, this was the iniquity of thy sister Sodom, pride, *fulness of bread*, and abundance of idleness was in her and in her daughters, *neither did she strengthen the hand of the poor and needy*. And they were haughty, and committed abomination before me..." (Ezekiel 16:49-50; *emphasis mine).*

The Bible offers specifications for overcoming gluttony and other fleshly desires.

- "And they that are Christ's have *crucified the flesh* with the affections and lusts" (Galatians 5:24; *emphasis mine*).
- "But I keep under my body, and *bring it under subjection*: lest that by any means, when I have preached to others, I myself should be a castaway" (1 Corinthians 9:27; *emphasis mine*).

- "Blessed are they which do **hunger and thirst after righteousness**: for they shall be filled" (Matthew 5:6; **emphasis mine**).
- "Whether therefore ye eat, or drink, or whatsoever ye do, **do all to the glory of God**" (1 Corinthians 10:31; **emphasis mine**).
- "But put ye on the Lord Jesus Christ, and **make not provision for the flesh, to fulfil the lusts thereof**" (Romans 13:14; **emphasis mine**).

According to the Word, we overcome our flesh by choosing salvation through Christ, by subjecting our flesh to the will of God, and by hungering after the things of God.

Final Thoughts

For most of us, we live in a world of opulence and luxury. We don't have to forage for food or go without because of lack. Let us stay grateful for the goodness of God and live contented, pursuing God above all else. This means we should not become greedy while living in the blessings of God.

If we're not careful, giving in to excess and pleasure will continue to be the norm, not only in the world but also in the church. Gluttony feeds our flesh and does not glorify God. We must die to our flesh, and that only happens when we submit ourselves to God and his authority. Setting aside food and other delicacies and seeking God will not only benefit our lives, but it will also benefit the church.

PART TWO
BIBLICAL INSIGHTS FOR A HOLY CHURCH

BIBLICAL INSIGHT #1:
FRUIT OF THE SPIRIT

But the fruit of the Spirit is love, joy, peace, longsuffering, gentleness, goodness, faith,

Meekness, temperance: against such there is no law (Galatians 5:22-23).

The Bible not only provides valuable warnings to protect us from the sins of worldly culture, but it also gives us the tools we need to follow Christ. I would be remiss if I did not illuminate biblical applications for God's church. We are not alone in this fight. We are not without a comforter, and he desires us to lean into him for strength, direction, and peace.

Seeking God first, as Jesus said in Matthew 6:33, is the starting point. When we pursue him above all else, everything else falls into place. And this deepening of our relationship with him will show up in our daily lives, specifically by the evidence of the fruit of the Spirit.

In Galatians, Paul discusses the fruit of the Spirit. Before we dig into the nine virtues described as fruit, we must first understand that having and exhibiting the fruit of the Spirit means we *must have* the Spirit, and we *must abide* in the vine, which is Jesus (John 15). Without the infilling of the Holy Ghost, we are empty vessels, walking in our flesh (Acts 2).

> *Even the mystery which hath been hid from ages and from generations, but now is made manifest to his saints: To whom God would make known what is the riches of the glory of this mystery among the Gentiles;* **which is Christ in you, the hope of glory:** *Whom we preach, warning every man, and teaching every man in all wisdom; that we may present* **every man perfect in Christ Jesus***: Whereunto I also labour, striving according to his working,* **which worketh in me mightily.** (Colossians 1:26-29; **emphasis mine**)

The key word in these verses is "in." Christ needs to be "in" us, and we need to be "in" him, so that he can work mightily "in" us. How does this happen?

We exhibit the fruit of the Spirit when we abide

"in" the vine. Jesus said, "I am the vine, ye are the branches: He that abideth in me, and I in him, the same bringeth forth much fruit: for without me ye can do nothing" (John 15:5). Therefore, the fruit of the Spirit operates when Christ dwells within us (through the Holy Ghost), and we are "in" Christ in our daily pursuit of our Savior. Doing so brings forth "much fruit."

Each fruit mentioned in Galatians 5 is vital in a holy church.

1. **Love:** Jesus made it clear that the first commandment is to love God before all else, and the second commandment is to love our neighbors. When we operate in love, we will be compassionate and kind, slow to anger.
2. **Joy:** According to Romans 15:13, God fills us with joy and peace so that we can have hope. This divinely given joy helps us in the trials and challenges of life. It brings a smile to our faces even if our world is in chaos because our hope is in Christ. And as Nehemiah 8:10 says, "The joy of the Lord is our strength…"

3. **Peace:** Joy and peace often go hand-in-hand because the joy of the Lord comes from his peace that passes understanding (Philippians 4:7). The peace found in God is a sense of calmness and continued hope regardless of current circumstances. It is worshipping God during trouble and staying humble and devoted to him when life doesn't make sense. God's peace protects us, and when we operate in his peace, we bring strength and serenity to situations that point others to him.
4. **Longsuffering:** Being slow to anger or offense is paramount in the church. People are imperfect, and patience is key when building Godly relationships. God is longsuffering toward us (Numbers 14:18; 2 Peter 3:9), and when we exhibit the fruit of the Spirit, we too need to follow his example by being patient with each other and quick to forgive.
5. **Gentleness:** This fruit of the spirit is built upon the foundation of humility (meekness). It is how we treat others and the world around us. This too means being patient with others and ourselves, but it

also means being kind and loving. It is an understanding that everyone has struggles in life and allows us to offer grace to each person instead of judging them harshly.

6. **Goodness:** When we are operating in God's goodness, we will walk in holiness and righteousness. This fruit of the Spirit is doing the right thing because it is right. It is loving God and his commandments and living out our relationship with him. Goodness is living a clean, moral life in such a way that others can see Christ in us. It is, therefore, the manifestation of all of the fruit of the Spirit operating in our lives.

7. **Faith:** This fruit of the Spirit is our trust and confidence in God. We believe in who he is and what his Word says. Operating in faith prevents the church from becoming dead because God responds to our faith.

8. **Meekness:** When pursuing Christ, we must humbly surrender to him. This same humility will show up in our lives, and it looks like serving others, submitting to God and Godly authority, and being open

to constructive criticism and opportunities for growth. This type of humility goes against the world's culture of pride, and it is beautiful in the eyes of the Lord (James 4:6; Luke 14:11; Proverbs 22:4). Meekness brings about gentleness.

9. **Temperance:** Self-control can be difficult, but when we pursue God first, his strength aids us in this type of submission. Temperance is practicing self-control every day in all areas. In a worldly culture that promotes "If it feels good, do it," Godly temperance is shunning lusts and pleasures. It is also connected to peace, longsuffering, and meekness because it keeps us from emotional outbursts or being quick to anger.

Operating in the fruit of the Spirit means dying daily to our flesh. But the effects of the fruit of the Spirit are too powerful to ignore. Hungry hearts searching for deliverance, salvation, peace, or something to add meaning to their lives will see Christ in us and want what we have. Revival starts with the fruit of the Spirit in the lives of the body of believers.

Final Thoughts

In all transparency, I still struggle to operate in all of the fruits of the Spirit. I can be quick to speak and slow to listen, and the Lord knows that patience is hard for me to exhibit.

1 Timothy 4:8 reminds us that godliness is profitable in all things. It starts and ends with God. I am encouraged because God's not done working on me. And the same is true for you. As long as we keep our eyes on him and submit to his will and Word, we can operate in the fruit of the Spirit and be more of an asset to the church and not a hindrance.

BIBLICAL INSIGHT #2:
UNITY OF THE SPIRIT

Endeavoring to keep the unity of the Spirit in the bond of peace (Ephesians 4:3).

There are more than 45,000 different Christian denominations around the world.[1] One Bible. One God. Yet 45,000 different interpretations of it?

There are several major divisions, and each of these divisions interpret Scripture differently. Then each division is broken down into more factions and divisions. Each of these denominations can then be separated into more micro-divisions within the division.[2]

For the nonbeliever, it is confusing. Which one is right? Is it like a fast-food restaurant where we pick the version we like best?

Christians have argued so much that they have killed each other for these differences. Millions of individuals have died because of persecution for their faith, and these were not always nonbelievers killing believers (even though that happened too).[3] Believers killed other believers who interpreted Scripture differently. Catholics killed Protestants, and Protestants killed Catholics.

But that was a long time ago, you may say. We don't kill each other anymore. We live peaceably together as the Bible dictates. Many Christians go so far as to say that our differences do not matter because we all believe in Jesus Christ as the Son of God who became the sacrificial lamb for all mankind. Yet, even within individual churches or denominations, there are disagreements and tension. The reality is as long as Satan keeps us divided, our spiritual growth will be stunted.

In Ephesians 4:4-6, Paul explains the need for unity because God is one:

There is one body, and one Spirit, even as ye are called in one hope of your calling; One Lord, one faith, one baptism, One God and Father of all, who is above all, and through all, and in you all.

There is only one way to God and that is through Jesus: "Jesus saith unto him, I am the way, the truth, and the life: no man cometh unto the Father, but by me" (John 14:6). When we choose Jesus as our Lord and Savior and are baptized in water and spirit, we become joint-heirs with Christ (Romans 8:17). One would think that unity of the Spirit would then become easy. Hardly so.

For the church to thrive and follow the commandments of the Word, unity of the Spirit is a necessity.

> *Now I beseech you, brethren, by the name of our Lord Jesus Christ, that **ye all speak the same thing, and that there be no divisions among you**; but that ye be **perfectly joined together** in the **same mind** and in the same judgment.* (1 Corinthians 1:10; **emphasis mine**)

We may question how to be of the same mind when each of us was raised differently and think differently. It is not easy to see eye-to-eye with people! Yet, Philippians 2:5 gives us the answer: we are to put on the mind of Christ. When we have him working inside of us, we are truly of one mind! Let's break this down further: What does unity of the Spirit in the church look like?

- Unity happens when peace is present. Peace among the believers happens when we follow Paul's instructions in Philippians 2:2:

"Fulfil ye my joy, that ye be likeminded, having the same love, being of one accord, of one mind."

- Unity happens with a thorough knowledge of who Jesus is through a relationship with him and a continued study of the Word.

"Till we all come in the unity of the faith, and of the knowledge of the Son of God, unto a perfect man, unto the measure of the stature of the fulness of Christ" (Ephesians 4:13).

- Unity happens when we come together for prayer and fasting.

"For where two or three are gathered together in my name, there am I in the midst of them" (Matthew 18:20).

- Unity happens when we humbly serve the kingdom of God.

"For we are labourers together with God: ye are God's husbandry, ye are God's building" (1 Corinthians 3:9).

- Unity happens with the breaking of bread and fellowship among the brothers and sisters in the Lord.

"Behold, how good and how pleasant it is for brethren to dwell together in unity" (Psalm 133:1).

- Unity happens when we extend the hand of friendship/fellowship to new members/converts.

"Finally, be ye all of one mind, having compassion one of another, love as brethren, be pitiful, be courteous" (1 Peter 3:8).

In the Book of Acts, the first church was on fire.

And when the day of Pentecost was fully come, **they were all with one accord in one place.** *And suddenly* *there came a sound from heaven as of a rushing mighty wind, and it filled all the house where they were sitting. And there appeared unto them cloven tongues like as of fire, and it sat upon each of them. And **they were all filled with the Holy Ghost**, and began to speak with other tongues, as the Spirit gave them utterance.* (Acts 2:1-4; **emphasis mine**)

Where there was unity, there was an outpouring of the Holy Ghost. Where there was unity, there were signs and wonders. Where there is unity of the Spirit, we open wide the doors for God's presence to come in.

Final Thoughts

Each of us has an important role to fill in the kingdom of God. Some of us are teachers, some are evangelists, some are pastors, etc. Yet, Paul tells us in Romans 12: 4-5 that we may have different roles to fill, but we are all one body:

For as we have many members in one body, and all members have not the same office: So we, being many, are one body in Christ, and every one members one of another. (Romans 12:4-5)

When the human body works in harmony with itself, great health and wholeness is the result. The same is true for the body of Christ. When God becomes our priority, unity of the Spirit is the result.

BIBLICAL INSIGHT #3:
SEPARATION FROM THE WORLD

And be not conformed to this world: but be ye transformed by the renewing of your mind, that ye may prove what is that good, and acceptable, and perfect, will of God. (Romans 12:2)

Most of us don't enjoy being different. Growing up, I endured bullying because I was a chubby church girl. Both of those details—being chubby and being a church girl—made me different enough to be the object of ridicule. Sometimes, blending in just seems easier, and it is. But that is not what God has required for his church.

If we are to be a holy church, there must be a proverbial line in the sand between kingdom culture and worldly culture. The church is not to look like or emulate the world. We are to be a city on a hill, not blending with the dominant cultural views.

> *But ye are a chosen generation, a royal priesthood, an holy nation, a peculiar people; that ye should shew forth the praises of him who hath called you out of darkness into his marvellous light; Which in time past were not a people, but are now the people of God: which had not obtained mercy, but now have obtained mercy.* (1 Peter 2:9-10)

This does not mean that there is arrogance in our demeanor or lifestyle, but when the lines blur to the point that the church and the world are indistinguishable, then the church has missed the mark. A holy church is called out, set apart.

- We are called to be clothed in humility.
- We are called to love others and serve in a way that gives God glory.
- We are called to be spotless. That means being washed in the blood of Christ through repentance, baptism in Jesus' name, and receiving His Spirit.

- We are called to be without blemish. This means that we walk away from sin, including fleshly desires that do not align with God's will.
- We shouldn't look like the world, speak like the world, or act like the world.
- We are called to exhibit the fruit of the Spirit because God is first in our lives.
- We are called to be unified together in "one mind" and "one accord" for the perfecting of the saints and for the work of the ministry.

This list is a tall order. We are human and are prone to error. But don't throw in the towel just yet. God is longsuffering toward us, and in our weakness, he is our strength. King David is an excellent example of this. He was an imperfect man, guilty of many sins, yet he pursued God above everything and was quick to repent of his wrongdoings. His relationship with God is highlighted throughout the Old Testament, specifically in his songs and poetry throughout the Books of Psalms. In the New Testament, Jesus offered compassion and mercy to those living sinful lifestyles, and doing so completely transformed their lives! Paul admonishes us to strive for the mastery, not for a "corruptible crown" but for an "incorruptible crown" (1 Corinthians 9:25). We're not "perfect" yet, but as long as we keep pursuing Jesus above all else, living a holy, righteous life is possible and needed in this present day.

Final Thoughts

As discussed in the introduction of this book, there are two cultures, and they are warring against each other. The same is true in our lives because we live in a fallen world, already born into sin. Yet, there is hope in Christ. This hope and salvation yank us out of the muck and mire of sin and darkness and set us on a straight and narrow path, one that leads to eternity in heaven.

We can, unfortunately, derail and stumble off course. This happens when our focus is on worldly desires and not on pursuing Christ. Paul encourages us in Colossians 3:2 to "Set your affection on things above, not on things on the earth." To accomplish this, we must separate ourselves from worldly lifestyles and the culture it glorifies. According to Romans 1:20, we are without excuse because God has revealed his truth to us.

When our treasures are in heaven, it's going to

make us different than the world. We're going to desire the things of God. And we can't draw closer to God while still feeding our flesh and giving in to fleshly impulses. When God increases in our lives, we will want more of him. And that is the church he desires.

EPILOGUE
A LETTER TO THE CHURCH

Dear Brothers and Sisters in Christ,

Life can be hard. Each of us endures our own struggles and disappointments. It's easy to lose focus and wander away from God's will for our lives. But we must remember who we are and who Jesus is!

- Don't be weary in well doing.
- Keep the faith.
- Hold fast to God's unchanging hand.

There is an old song that I remember singing in church when I was younger. The chorus—written by Dottie Rambo—is:

> I'm talking about the church in the book of Revelation
> It's built on the rock, it's got a firm foundation,
> It's been through the flood, and it's been through the fire,
> And one of these days, this church is gonna move up higher,
> It's the church...triumphant, Oh Lord, and it's built by the hand of the Lord.[1]

The church has fought spiritual warfare against worldly culture since it began. It flies in the face of what the world promotes and endorses. But we must not give in to the pressure to mold ourselves after the world because people need Jesus.

The world needs us to shine the light of God's grace and compassion. Masses of humanity are depressed, angry, alone, and longing for the peace and hope that can only be found through God. We have work to do. The world needs the church. The world needs you and me.

Sincerely,
Your sister in Christ

NOTES

INTRODUCTION

1. Amy Watson, May 23, 2022. Bible Readership in the U.S. 2018-2021. Statista.com

CHAPTER 1

1. Josue Glausiusz, Living in an Imaginary World, January 1, 2014. Scientific American, https://www.scientificamerican.com/article/living-in-an-imaginary-world/

CHAPTER 3

1. Michael W. Smith, Friends, 1983.

CHAPTER 6

1. Jeffrey M. Jones, U.S. Church Membership Down Sharply in Past Two Decades, April 18, 2019. Gallup. https://news.gallup.com/poll/248837/church-membership-down-sharply-past-two-decades.aspx
2. The State of Church Attendance: Trends and Statistics [2023]. Church Trac. https://www.churchtrac.com/articles/the-state-of-church-attendance-trends-and-statistics-2023
3. Aaron Earls. Apathy in Churches Looms Large for Pastors. May 10, 2022. Lifeway Research. https://research.lifeway.-

com/2022/05/10/apathy-in-churches-looms-large-for-pastors...

CHAPTER 9

1. Alan J. Steinberg, M.D. What is Pleasure? Psychology Today. March 12, 2022. https://www.psychologytoday.com/us/blog/the-meditating-mind/202203/what-is-pleasure...
2. Josh Herring, Fast Forward, 2021.

BIBLICAL INSIGHT #2:

1. Donavyn Coffey, July 29, 2022. Why Does Christianity Have So Many Denominations? Live Science. https://www.livescience.com/christianity-denominations.html...
2. Mary Fairchild. June 25, 2019. Development of Christian Denominations. Learn Religions. https://www.learnreligions.com/christian-denominations-700530
3. Dan Wooding. Modern Persecution. May 3, 2010. Christianity.com. https://www.christianity.com/church/church-history/timeline/1901-2000/modern-persecution-11630665.html

EPILOGUE

1. Dottie Rambo, It's the Church Triumphant.

Thank you for reading and supporting this work by Janice Broyles.

Please read her other nonfiction works:

No Longer Rejected:

A Woman's Journey from Rejection to Freedom

Expecting Greater:

Aligning Our Desires with God's Will

Please read her fiction works:

The Secret Heir *(a Biblical Retelling of David)*

The Runaway Heir *(Book #2: a Biblical Retelling of David)*

The Anointed Heir *(Book #3: a Biblical Retelling of David)*

www.ingramcontent.com/pod-product-compliance
Lightning Source LLC
Chambersburg PA
CBHW071456080526
44587CB00014B/2121